TRUTH DECAY

A Call for Accountability & Transparency in the Adventist Church

Albert C. Koppel, DDS

TRUTH DECAY

A Call for Accountability
& Transparency
in the
Adventist Church

By Albert C. Koppel, DDS

TRUTH DECAY

FIRST EDITION
Copyright © 2005 by
Albert C. Koppel, DDS

ISBN 0-7880-2162-1

PRINTED IN U.S.A.

TRUTH DECAY

Dedication

To the memory of my
German (Hungarian born) father,
Karl Koppel (1887 – 1992),
who trusted implicitly the "Yes, Brother Koppel"
assurances of the brethren who he believed
would assure the greatest benefit possible
for the Church he loved.

Acknowledgements

I thank my wife, Betty, for her continual support and careful reading of multiple generations of proofs as we painstakingly wrote, checked, rewrote, rechecked, added, and deleted, with few pauses over a period of more than 18 months. I am also deeply indebted to my literary assistant and publisher, Edwin A. Schwisow, whose encouragement in this project and grace with the English language transformed my musings into a coherent manuscript. I also thank Ron Burgard of MacMouser Graphics for his patience and creativity in designing this complicated book. To my many friends and fellow church members, pastors, conference presidents, and world Church leaders who offered their help and suggestions, I extend my thanks. And, finally, I thank those denominational leaders, some cited by position in these pages, who read the first complete draft and added helpful context, including Nate Schilt of Loma Linda University. Without the help of all of you, this book could never be.

TRUTH DECAY
Table of Contents

Preface . . .

An American Family's Success

By Robert J. Szana, DDS

Al and Betty Koppel

*A*s a dentist, my friend Al Koppel knows all about tooth decay. And as a member of the Seventh-day Adventist Church, he knows about Truth Decay—the loss of forthrightness, full disclosure, openness, and integrity.

In briefly sharing his life story in the pages to come, he's made it clear to me that his compelling goal is to share the truth, the whole truth, and nothing but the truth. I know it's often been difficult and even embarrassing for him, but he's done his best, because he believes in his Church and wants to see it become an even better Church than it is today.

Albert Charles Koppel was born at home in New York City, November 26, 1918. His father had immigrated to the United States in 1910. His mother was born in 1897 in the United States to parents native to Alsace Lorraine.

Al's parents and maternal grandparents became Seventh-day Adventists after landing on these shores. All were members of the Gates Avenue Seventh-day Adventist Church in Brooklyn, New York.

He spent his first six years of life in New York, where he began attending church school and learned English and German—both at the same time.

Koppel family

When Al was six, his parents moved to central New Jersey, where he finished grade school in the Trenton Church School. There, his parents operated two businesses—the Universal Knitting Mill and Universal Farms. His father enjoyed the outdoors and managed the farm; Mom managed the mill, in addition to being cook, housekeeper, wife, and mother.

Al had two younger brothers, Ural and Lawrence —neither of whom reached middle age. Lawrence succumbed to head injuries sustained in a tragic bicycle accident, at age 14. Ural (whose intended name was Uriah, but was misspelled on his birth certificate as Urial and was eventually simplified to "Ural") grew to adulthood, married, and worked on the farm with Pop until his untimely death at age 39, of cancer.

The death of the 14-year-old Lawrence was particularly hard on Al's mother, but even in her grief, she tried to shield her oldest son from the trauma of Lawrence's passing. Since Al was taking final exams in dental school at the time of Lawrence's death, she did not want to distract him from his studies, so waited until his return home a few days later to break the terrible news.

Al's first experience as a student away from home came at North Plainfield Academy, in 1931 and 1932. Then, encouraged by New Jersey Conference president, H.J. Detweiler, Al enrolled in Shenandoah Valley Academy—

Betty Adams, graduation from College of Medical Evangelists

a boarding school in Virginia, 300 miles from his home.

Twenty miles south of the Koppels' residence in Robbinsville, just three months after Al was born in New York, a daughter had arrived in the Herbert Adams home. Sarah Elizabeth "Betty" Adams attended public grade school and completed her first three years of high school in Burlington, New Jersey.

Then, Betty succeeded in getting her parents' approval to attend Shenandoah Valley Academy for the 1934-1935 school year. There, she and Al, both 16, graduated together in the Class of 1935.

He was a shy 16, and during that school year, after being assured by Betty's close girlfriend that she would accept, he mustered the courage to ask her for a date on Class Night.

They both attended Columbia Junior College, where Betty enrolled as a pre-med student. After two years, she applied to the College of Medical Evangelists (now Loma Linda University) in Loma Linda, California. She was turned down because she was only 18 but a year later was admitted. She graduated as a physician at age 23, at the top of the middle third of her class.

Meanwhile, Al took a detour that put him a year behind Betty. But a year later, he also applied to the College of Medical Evangelists, but was not accepted.

When Al told his father that he thought his grades may have been incorrectly transmitted, his father said, "Here is a thousand dollars. Go out to Loma Linda. You might get in anyway."

His father ("Pop," as he was known) was right. As

soon as Al spoke to the registrar and clarified the transcript situation, he was admitted, and he and Betty renewed their friendship by way of Friday-evening walks through the palm-treed lanes of Loma Linda.

Hired help digging potatoes during the 1930s. Several decades later the Robbinsville Adventist Church was built here.

The Karl Koppel farm produces a bumper crop of strawberries in its prime.

Pop had often told Al he was "dumb," because Al didn't excel in mechanical skills and welding, as his younger brother did. And Pop's evaluation had taken its psychological toll.

The mass of material a medical student faces can be overwhelming. Al studied hard during those first weeks of medical school—harder than he had ever studied in his life. But the results of his first Anatomy examination came back with a grade of 27 percent. Pop's words echoed in his ears: "Dumb! Dumb!" (Al later learned that the class average for that particular test was the same as his—27 percent.)

Koppel's large potato storage building in the 1960s. He donated it to the Conference.

Convinced he was a failure, Al quit medical school and boarded a Greyhound bus back to the East Coast—the longest, most depressing ride of his life. What would become of him? He didn't know. But of one thing he was sure: He would never again hear from Betty Adams.

He went back to work on the family farm, but his father, disappointed by Al's failure in medical school, refused to speak to him for five years. Pop took Al's failure personally—as if Al had failed him. With only a ninth-grade education, Pop clearly was anxious to achieve some of his own ambitions through Al's success. But Al had let him down!

Miracle of miracles, however, one day soon after returning to New Jersey, Al received a sensitively written letter from Betty. In it, she let him know he still had value as a person and that in her eyes he had committed no sin.

When spring came, Al's mother suggested that he drive down to Atlanta and visit several college friends who were studying dentistry at Atlanta-Southern Dental College. Al made the trip and attended classes with them for a few days. Still lacking self-confidence, at the end of each day of classes, Al would ask his friends to listen as he played back from memory a summary of what the instructors had taught.

When his friends assured him that he had it all straight, Al grew confident that he might be able to survive as a dental student. So he applied and was accepted.

Meanwhile, his estrangement with his father continued, and Pop refused to help with Al's expenses. But his mother scraped and saved and devoted $2,000 to his education from an inheritance she had recently received when her mother died.

When Church leaders learned that Pop was not speaking to Al, they too tried to help. Many years later, Al learned that physician Henry Hadley, Sr., had attempted to convince "Brother Koppel" to help his son financially. Dr. Hadley had assured Pop that dentistry was also an honorable profession. But Pop had answered, "Thousands for medical school but not a cent for dentistry."

Andrew Fearing held evangelistic meetings in the city of Trenton during that period of time, and he talked and prayed with Pop Koppel about his relationship with Al. Many years later, Fearing became a patient in Al's dental practice, and one day he said to Al, "I'm surprised that you are still in the Church."

Karl Koppel with wife Katherine. She knew him as Karl, but in business matters he preferred "Charles."

But I'm getting ahead of the story. One of the first things students were given to do in dental school was to carve a tooth out of a block of plaster. Al says he had never even carved a whistle out of a piece of wood, and he was sure he would fail.

But as he sat at the long work bench with the other students, carving away, one of the dentists, an instructor in dental anatomy, put his hand on Al's shoulder and in his southern drawl, said, "Dahktah, you're doing a good job."

The instructor seemed honest, and confidence and determination shot through Al like an injection of adrenalin. From that day forward, his grades improved, as he tried even harder to excel. Four years later, he would graduate 14th in his class of 103. He was the only student in his class to take the National Board Examinations in Dentistry that year.

In the meantime, Betty and Al continued their correspondence. She was about to graduate from medical school and had already accepted an internship at the 3,000-bed Los Angeles County Hospital. In Al's next letter, he asked her if she had ever considered taking an internship in the South. Her answering letter brought the news: "I have one." Al was delighted that she had found a way to intern at Atlanta's Piedmont Hospital.

By this time Al was about halfway through his dental education. His confidence was back and he knew Betty loved him. He was on "Cloud Nine."

It was at this point, about 62 years ago, that Al's and my paths crossed. We discovered we had somewhat similar heritages. My parents were both natives of Hungary.

Although Pop Koppel had a German heritage, he had been born and reared in Hungary and spoke fluent Hungarian.

But now, back to Al's story. When Betty arrived in Atlanta, via New Jersey, she brought with her a hefty dose of reality, in the form of Al's Draft Board induction papers. Al's heart sank—surely, this was the end of all good things. But life took a turn for the better, a few days later, when the mail brought him a Medical Administrative Corps 2nd Lieutenant's commission for the US Army.

This meant Al would be on an inactive commission— a classification arranged to keep students of the health professions, like Al, in school until they graduated. So he wrote his Draft Board and advised them that he now was a 2nd Lieutenant in the United States Army Medical Administrative Corps. (Of historical note, during our time in Atlanta, an internist Betty served under was called to the Little White House in Georgia when President Roosevelt died. The physician knew the back roads of Georgia and made the trip in record time.)

Betty and Al were married October 2, 1942, by Pastor Lindsay Semmons, who had taught them both at Columbia Junior College. When Betty had asked him to perform their marriage, she'd reminded him of two pieces of advice he'd given her before she'd entered medical school: "Don't drink coffee to stay up late and study, and watch out for those medical students." She'd followed his counsel, she said, but would he please marry her to this dental student?

When Betty finished her internship, the anesthesiologists at Piedmont Hospital asked her to join their department, where she took training in anesthesiology until Al graduated from dental school on August 30, 1944. The specialty Betty "fell into" later proved to be a tremendous blessing in Al's dental practice.

Now they moved to the nation's capital, where they rented an apartment in Takoma Park, Maryland, for $55 a month.

Betty administered anesthesia at Washington Sanitarium & Hospital during the day and worked nights in anesthesiology at Columbia Hospital for Women, just a few city blocks from the White House.

By now, soldiers were coming home from World War II and the baby business was thriving; sometimes she administered anesthesia for as many as 10 deliveries a night. Later (1953) Betty would spend a year at Harvard's Massachusetts General Hospital in an anesthesia residency, under the supervision of Dr. Bernard Briggs, a man she much admires and who later chaired the department of anesthesiology at Loma Linda University.

But in the meantime, the two beat-up cars Betty and Al were driving both gave out, and they didn't know what to do. So Al spoke to H. J. Detweiler, Potomac Conference president and former president of the New Jersey Conference, and told him about their situation.

Since Pop was a substantial donor to the Church, Al knew that his estranged relationship with his father was no secret to Detweiler. So Detweiler immediately said, "Albert, you need to have a reliable car," and arranged for the Conference to loan Al and Betty the necessary funds.

News of the loans soon got back to Pop, of course, and placed Pop in the unenviable position of being a big contributor to the Church, while Church leaders were loaning Al money. But more about that later.

Dr. Hadley, who had attempted unsuccessfully to reconcile Pop with his son some years before, helped Al get a 12-month internship in Oral Surgery at Garfield Memorial Hospital under Dr. Karl Hayden Wood (1944). Each morning, Al wired fractured jaws, extracted teeth, and surgically removed impacted wisdom teeth. Many patients also came to the clinic to have roots from broken teeth removed.

Then, afternoons, Al worked in Dr. Wood's Oral Surgery practice in the high-rise medical office building at

1835 Eye Street, NW. After only three months, Dr. Wood went on vacation to Florida, leaving Al to run the office.

Dr. Wood, it turned out, at one time had studied theology at Atlantic Union College, but gave that up to study pharmacy, then dentistry. Finally he'd specialized in oral surgery. Active in dental society politics, for a year he had served as president of the District of Columbia Dental Society.

Al followed his mentor's example, and from 1945 to 1946, studied in the University of Pennsylvania Graduate School, Department of Oral Surgery.

Though Al would eventually practice dentistry for 40 years in one location, at that time he thought he might want to move about in his career, so he took the licensing examinations in New Jersey, Maryland, Washington, D.C., Virginia, Georgia, and California.

But Al was technically still a 2nd Lieutenant, and the Medical Administrative Corps required him to apply, upon graduation, for a commission in the United States Army Dental Corps. So he presented himself at Walter Reed Army Medical Center for physical examination.

The examining physician asked him if he had any physical disabilities. Al replied, "No," but said his right shoulder sometimes would slip out of joint.

"Then you're out," the physician declared. Clearly the war would end soon, and the army had little need for new officers.

Relieved, Al began looking around for business opportunities and learned that Ernest Woolgar, a 77-year-old Adventist dentist, was thinking about selling his home and office. So Al again called on Potomac Conference President Detweiler and asked him to accompany him to talk with the elderly dentist.

After they had inspected the residence/office, dental equipment, and practice, located just inside the District of Columbia-Maryland line, Detweiler asked Dr. Woolgar what he was asking for the practice, building, and equipment. Dr. Woolgar said $21,000.

Detweiler then turned to Al and said, "Albert, that seems like a fair price. Why don't you give Dr. Woolgar a deposit?"

"Elder Detweiler, I don't have any money," Al truthfully replied.

"You have a dollar, don't you?" Detweiler urged. So, at Detweiler's direction, Al handed Dr. Woolgar a dollar bill and the dentist gave Al a receipt.

It all happened so quickly, Al felt dazed, wondering if he had done the right thing. And it didn't help that the very next day, Dr. Woolgar phoned and offered to buy back the $1 receipt for $500! What to do?

Al decided to take no chances: "Dr. Woolgar, let me talk to Elder Detweiler about this," he said.

Detweiler told Al he would speak to Dr. Woolgar, and Al later learned that Detweiler had called the dentist and bluntly asked, "Why, Brother Woolgar, you wouldn't go back on your word, would you?"

Taken aback, Dr. Woolgar quickly agreed that a deal was a deal, and Al came to acquire his first, and only, dental practice.

The Koppels had this home built in the depths of the Great Depression for $8,000.

Adventist pastors have played pivotal roles in Al's life. He often tells the boyhood story of seeing a car approach as he cultivated a field of potatoes. Under the shroud of dust, he'd recognized his pastor, driving out to meet him. Pastors' visits to the Koppel farm were by no means unusual, and Al had learned that those visits often included requests for contributions.

So as the pastor approached, Al had called out over the

din of the tractor that his Pop was in the other field. But the pastor kept coming and got out of his car, so Al swung down from the tractor to greet the man of God. After the pleasantries, the pastor said, "Albert, I came to

Robert Boggess, former New Jersey Conference president, confers with Karl Koppel. Koppel in life counted many Church leaders as personal friends.

see *you*. How are you getting along spiritually?"

He then put his arm around Al and prayed for him, right there next to the tractor. Al was impressed and moved. To think that a pastor would drive out in the field and get his car dusty just to see him!

Little wonder that Al developed tremendous admiration for Church leaders, who encouraged him with their time and good counsel, and even assisted him financially when he really needed it. This high regard, he says, makes writing this book difficult, but all the more necessary.

As Al prepared to open his dental office in Takoma Park, little did he realize that one day he would be known by at least one denominational employee as "the Unofficial Official Dentist" for the General Conference and nearby Review & Herald Publishing Association.

Al owes his very livelihood in many ways to the Adventist people and their leaders, and during his more than 40 years of dental practice, his relationship with his Adventist clients was always cordial.

As Al set out to renovate his office after buying the practice, he employed Opha Mays, an Adventist Church member, to do the work. He asked Mays what he would do if Al couldn't pay him. Mays said, "Oh, you will pay me." He had more confidence in Al than Al had in himself!

And as it turned out, so many dentists were still in the army that Al had a full appointment book the day he opened the office.

Al hated debt and, worse yet, hated paying interest. So, he reduced his indebtedness as quickly as possible. Only after his first dental operatory was paid for did he consider purchasing a second one.

Since the office was only about four city blocks from the offices of the General Conference of Seventh-day Adventists, many Adventist leaders and their family members soon became his patients. And word of Al's success was getting back to Pop Koppel.

Pop apparently believed that Al had done at least one thing right in life: He had married the right "girl"! He liked his daughter-in-law, so after about five years of silence, he started speaking to Al again. When Betty and Al drove Pop and Mom to Florida for a winter vacation, Pop asked Al how much he still owed on his home and office. Al told Pop the truth—$10,000.

On the spot, Pop offered to buy out the mortgage at a low rate of interest. So Betty and Al drafted a note payable for $10,000. When Al handed him the note, Pop returned it to him and told him to simply put it in his safe.

When, a year later, Al asked Pop what he wanted him to do with that $10,000 note, Pop told him to tear it up. Things were definitely thawing in the Koppel family!

But things were cold as ice on the international scene, as capitalism and Communism vied for dominance. When the Korean Conflict erupted, Al was "called up" immediately.

He closed his office and reported to Fort Sam Houston, Texas, where the army did its best for six weeks to turn Al and 450 other dentists and physicians into officers in the US Army Dental and Medical Corps.

Finally, the day came for duty assignment. An army general, a dentist, announced that he was looking for five dental officers with experience in oral surgery. Al joined the line of officers with oral surgery experience, and when it came his turn to be interviewed, Al told the general about his professional experience in oral surgery, concluding that he had also worked in the office of Dr. Karl Hayden Wood, in Washington, D.C.

"Oh, you know Karl?" the General smiled. "Stand over here."

And so it was that Al became one of the five oral surgeons chosen for assignment in the European Command in Germany. The remaining 70 dental officers all went to Korea.

Al told me, "It turned out, my tour of duty was more like a good vacation. When the Service is nice, it's nice, but when it's bad, it's really bad!"

Al and Betty later became parents of two daughters— Karla Rae and Marsha Fay. Karla Rae Morrill is today a medical transcriptionist in Maine; Marsha Fay Nagel is a registered nurse (B.S.) in Loma Linda, Calif., and has masters' degrees in religion and public health.

Pop had once vowed "not a cent for dentistry." But a few years after Al returned to his office from Germany, Al asked his father to match his $1,000 gift (that was when a thousand dollars was worth a thousand dollars!) to the brand-new Loma Linda University School of Dentistry. His Pop did!

The fact that Al had just served as a visiting instructor in the new school's Oral Surgery Department may have had something to do with his Pop's sudden enthusiasm for his son's vocation. Pop Koppel was by now proud of how well Al was doing in dentistry.

When Pop reached 100 years of age, Al reminded him that when he was young he had told Al he was "dumb" because he was not handy in mechanical areas. Al also reminded him that when he would send him and his brother to the New York Markets, each with a load of potatoes, Al invariably would sell his load first and Al's brother would then say, "Albey, let me take your truck home and you sell the rest of my load."

Al saw the wheels turning in Pop's head as he reflected that Al was better with money than his brother had been. And Al was amazed that as Pop got older, he allowed him to handle several large financial matters for him.

Leaving medical school had been extremely traumatic for Al. But he has enjoyed and loved the practice of dentistry—so much so that he never thought of it as work. And, as a dentist, he enjoyed a better home and family life than most physicians. Rarely did he have to return to the office after working hours.

He thanks the Lord for the good life he and Betty have had. Their marriage has lasted more than 62 years. And for that, he is humbly thankful and—well, just plain proud!

Al's membership in the National Association of Seventh-day Adventist Dentists (NASDAD) dates back to 1943, the year after NASDAD was organized. He served as Secretary/Treasurer and in 1955 was elected President of NASDAD.

Al is also a life member of the American Dental Association, the District of Columbia Dental Society.

In the mid 1970s, the following item appeared in The District of Columbia Dental Society's Newsletter:

"On November 8, Dr. Albert Koppel will be honored as a recipient of the Mastership in the Academy of General Dentistry, the most coveted award this group bestows. Dr. Koppel received his Fellowship from the Academy in 1965, the first District of Columbia dentist to be so honored and with the coming presentation shall be the first and only recipient of the Mastership in Washington, D.C. The Mastership degree signifies an overall competence in all fields of General Dentistry and is equivalent to what may be considered as specialization in the field of general dentistry. Dr. Koppel is a credit and an honor to our profession."

The following appraisal of the Academy of General Dentistry's Mastership Award appeared in one of the journals of the Loma Linda University School of Dentistry:

"Two School of Dentistry alumni were among six general practitioners in California who earned the Academy of General Dentistry's prestigious Mastership Award ... It is not an easy task to accomplish this, according to the Academy. First, one must achieve fellowship status by completing 500 course hours within ten years and then pass a written examination. The road to Mastership involves 600 additional hours, 400 of which must be earned by participating in hands-on courses sanctioned by the AGD. There are in excess of 100,000 dentists in the United States, and only about 1,400 have achieved Mastership status since they were first awarded in 1972."

Needless to say, Al is also a lifelong, committed member of the Seventh-day Adventist Church, and he and his wife have been unstinting in their support of their Church. But as they became involved in giving larger and larger sums to the Church, they uncovered serious credibility problems within the Church's Trust Services program.

As a dentist, Dr. Koppel understands well the problems of *Tooth Decay* and it's preventive cure—Fluoride. He and I both believe this book will help the Seventh-day Adventist Church identify areas of long-hidden administrative *Truth Decay*. Al wants to help the Church rebuild problem areas where trust and faith among members have eroded, due to carelessness and mismanagement.

I urge you to give careful and prayerful consideration to his story and its Epilogue.

Robert J. Szana, D.D.S.
2005

Chapter 1

TRUTH DECAY

In Seventh-day Adventist Schools

*A*s a young man, I'd learned to love the Seventh-day Adventist Church and its leaders. And by and large, I still do. But there's another side to Adventism—the institutional side—that can be as cold and calculating as the everyday fellowship is warm and inviting. My first brush with the profound secrecy and defensive reticence of the institutional Church came early in my adult life.

My daughters had reached the sixth and seventh grades, respectively, at the John Nevins Andrews (JNA) Grade School, in Takoma Park, Maryland. Our school was overflowing with offspring and relatives of high Church leadership, and we believed it to be one of the best Adventist church schools in the world.

The highly capable daughter of well-known Jewish Seventh-day Adventist Church leader F.C. Gilbert was the principal. We felt fortunate indeed!

One evening, I happened to pick up my daughters' literature book, titled *Counterpoint in Literature*, and began thumbing through it.

As I skimmed through the selections, I was surprised— then appalled—to find the Lord's name taken in vain—not once, but many times. One part, as I remember it after almost 40 years, tells the unbelievable story of a father wringing off the head of his daughter's kitty. Another tells of a Sicilian man who punishes his disobedient son by killing him. The commentary suggests that before we judge these fathers too harshly, we try to understand their cultural backgrounds.

Coming from a generation of men and women that instinctively honors authority, defends and supports teachers, and earnestly exhorts their children to "study to show yourselves approved," I didn't know how best to express my concerns about the textbook.

Certainly, this was not the best possible literature for my 11- and 12-year-old daughters! But I said nothing to my daughters about my concerns. I wanted to do nothing to denigrate their school, or instructors, in their eyes, as I pondered how to handle the situation.

Then, one day as I ambled through a shopping mall, waiting for my wife to make her purchases, in the window of a Christian bookstore I noticed a title, "Textbooks on Trial."

It was a report of the battle of a Christian couple, Mel and Norma Gabler, to have morally objectionable textbooks removed from public schools. So I bought the book and wrote a letter to the authors, asking their opinion of my daughters' textbook, *Counterpoint in Literature.*

In turn, they sent me an inch-thick document with their appraisal of the book, highlighting passages where it seemed to condone ideas and practices out of harmony with Christian principles.

"So what we have here is a simple mistake," I thought. "Our school board doesn't realize all that this book contains." I resolved to share my findings with them, without accusation or condemnation.

About that time, Louise Klueser, then a member of the Ministerial Department of the General Conference, came to my dental office for treatment, and I asked her how she thought I should handle the problem.

"Do what the Bible says—go to the individual responsible," she replied. "Then, if that fails, go to the principal and on up the chain of command."

So I met with the literature teacher, but she told me she had no authority to change textbooks at that point in the year. So, I made an appointment to speak with the JNA principal.

Apparently she had been forewarned of my concern, for when I entered her office, she greeted me, "Doctor, what is this about your going to get rid of me?" I answered truthfully, "Mrs. _____ , those words have never crossed my lips; in fact, the thought has never even crossed my mind."

In her eyes, the textbook issue seemed to suggest something deeper, more sinister. And she refused to discuss my concerns—or for that matter to defend the book, itself. We were getting nowhere.

So I phoned the Potomac Conference secretary of education and found that he too had a prepared speech (word had apparently gotten through that I was on a witch hunt to bring down one of the conference's most valued teachers.)

Without preamble, he challenged me, "Doctor, perhaps you would be more comfortable moving your children to another school."

What! Move my children from one of the best schools in the denomination? I was only trying to help my school do an even better job!

But what came across to me that day was a clear message that I was a parent and they were the educators. And there was nothing I could say that could possibly help them do a better job. If I didn't like the way they were doing things, I could take my business elsewhere.

My wife and I were shaken to the core. I had been taught, as a child, that Christians are to be "servant leaders," open, understanding, and patient with those seeking truth. We'd just been told to "put up, or be quiet." And—dutiful church members that we were—we ended up doing both.

But it taught us a lesson—that high-sounding words about "servant leadership" are no substitute for the real thing. We determined in our lives never to allow ourselves to treat others as we had been treated.

Which is why I am writing this book with care, and above all else, prayer—and why I've waited so many years to publish it.

We have a wonderful Church with Bible-based doctrines and a good school system. But in so many cases, we more than cancel out these strengths by the way we treat one another. I have been immensely pleased that in more recent times, we are seeing a far greater emphasis in our Church on the importance of relationships.

If we're really serious about the high levels of apostasy among our youth, the fracturing of our congregations into independent movements, and the declining effect of public evangelism, it's high time we took a long, hard look at how we treat one another.

It's not all due to "a changing world." A lot of it has to do with our tenacious determination to "defeat" dissenters. It's depleting our Church from within and minimizing our impact on society. And, sad to say, our experience with the literature book was but a foretaste of far more serious trials to come.

Chapter 2

TRUTH DECAY

Regarding Seventh-day Adventist Higher Education

*M*y wife, Betty, and I have supported Adventist education and are grateful alumni of Washington Missionary College (now Columbia Union College.) If I can help move Adventist education forward to greater good, that's my prayer as I write these words.

Life moved on for our family, and in time my daughters were out of school, married, and one had a daughter of her own. As life would have it, we were nearing 65 years of age—that golden time of life when men and women suddenly collapse into rockers to coddle those wonderful grandkids!

But just as we were preparing to retire, the situation in the home of one daughter required that our then-three-year-old granddaughter come to live with us. Our home became her home, and it seemed only a short time, to me, and she was ready to go to college.

We'd moved to the Shenandoah Valley of Virginia to retire, and we did not want our granddaughter to study in a local college. So she chose to attend Columbia Union College. We couldn't tell her "No."

Though she lived in the College dormitory, she often came home on weekends. One evening at home, she put a videotape in our VCR and began watching a profanity-laced movie about a female reporter who lived a promiscuous lifestyle.

"Kathy," I asked, "what are you watching?"

"My homework!" she replied.

The next week she phoned home and reported that a teacher had told the class that sending American missionaries to work in foreign lands was wrong—that it disturbed local cultures!

"Kathy," I asked, "do you know what the name of Columbia Union College was before it became CUC?

"No," she replied.

"It was called Washington Missionary College," I said. "And if you believe what your teacher says about missionaries, are you ready to throw out the Gospel commission that tells us to 'Go'?"

"No," she said. She wasn't ready to do that.

But she did tell me that a female professor had taken her and a group of her friends to watch a film in a theater. And when Valentines Day rolled around, we learned that the College bus had been used to transport CUC students to an auditorium in a nearby town, where they were given dancing instruction. Later that year, students traveled on that same bus to attend an opera in Baltimore—an opera that featured the devil and presented him in a fairly good light, according to my granddaughter. Things had definitely changed at College since we'd been there!

So I wrote a letter to the Columbia Union president, who was also the chairman of the Columbia Union College Board, expressing my concerns. Five weeks later he phoned and told me he'd received my letter and had spoken to the Columbia Union College and Potomac Conference presidents. Then the phone went silent.

I waited for a long time and, finally, embarrassed, asked, "Are you finished?"

"Yes," he said.

"Then, when can we expect change in these things?"

"I can't tell you that," he replied.

"What, then," I asked, "is the proper way for me, a constituent member of the Columbia Union Conference and a financial sponsor of a CUC student, to protest the things I've seen and heard?"

Again, silence. He would not answer, and I was left to conclude that there was no normal protocol—no established way—for parents and relatives to comment on what their loved ones were being taught at the College.

So I pressed him a bit and asked him if he didn't think that integrity demanded that the College marketing department explain to prospective students and their parents that not all instruction and social events condoned by the College complied with traditional Adventist standards.

"We can't do that," the Union president replied. And after more moments of embarrassing silence, our conversation ended.

I was flabbergasted! Adventist pastors and administrators frequently quote Ellen White's pithy advice: "The greatest want of the world is the want of men—men who will not be bought or sold; men who in their inmost souls are true and honest, men who do not fear to call sin by its right name, men whose conscience is as true to duty as the needle to the pole" (*Education*, 57). This is what they teach, but when we ask that a college's marketing materials be honest and forthright in portraying the spiritual fare our children will be fed, we are told, "We can't do that."

I realize that as Christians, we do our best to live "in the world" without being part "of the world." And the way we go about living that distinction can vary from situation to situation, from generation to generation.

But we must learn to dialogue, to discuss, and to handle these sticky questions openly and honestly. And now, in the education of our granddaughter, we were experiencing that same truculent, stone-faced, resistant behavior we had endured 35 years before, when our own daughters were still in grade school.

Somehow, Adventist educators appear to have been taught that if an earnest parent or student raises uncomfortable, controversial questions about policy, that good educators should . . .

1. Switch the subject.
2. Refuse to give a direct answer, or
3. Ignore the petitioner and his questions.

Granted, dealing with children and their demanding parents is no easy occupation, and I sympathize deeply with our teachers. But they could save themselves and the Church so much grief if they could learn to . . .

1. Anticipate concerns,
2. Address those concerns before they fester into confrontations, and
3. If confrontations occur, dignify the earnest questioners with intelligent dialogue and a course of thoughtful resolution.

The inability of our churches, schools, and colleges to master these skills has only compounded the rumors swirling around our institutions. During the past 30 years, most colleges have invested heavily in hiring public relations and marketing staff—many serving under the guise of "alumni relations" and "advancement" personnel.

Certainly our institutions can benefit from better alumni relations and financial advancement. But in a sense, we're barricading a barn with no horse inside.

So many of us have been treated for so long with silence and condescension, it's often hard for us to defend our Church. A General Conference vice president recently told me, "Unfortunately, our schools are no longer the havens of refuge they once were."

Maybe he's wrong! I hope he's wrong! Maybe in their own way, despite the occasional mistake and oversight, our colleges and schools remain true to their calling. But the case seems thin indeed, when the prevailing treatment of dissenters is essentially a "no comment, we're not going to talk about your concerns."

Little wonder that an attorney on Church payroll recently told me, "When I sent my boys to Seventh-day

Adventist schools, I did so knowing that it was the lesser of two evils." And smaller wonder still that a whole new genre of education is emerging—a so-called "self-supporting" system that in its own way is attempting to fill the needs of those students and parents who have said, "Enough!" More and more Adventist families are opting to home-school their children, including such men as prominent Adventist broadcaster Doug Batchelor.

It isn't surprising , then, that a February 2004 report on Adventist higher education in the *Adventist Review* depicts conditions as "Sobering."

If solutions to this "sobering" situation are to be found, we must begin by asking leaders to put aside their elitist, dismissive behavior and do a better job accounting for the trends they allow in our schools.

In the April 11, 2004, issue of *Adventist Review*, I found that I am not alone in my concerns. In her article, "The Most Popular Adventist Sin," Evelyn Caro writes, "Members need to become acquainted with the biblical requirements for Church leadership, *so they can hold leaders accountable to them* (italics mine)."

Fortunately, not all is lost—we're beginning to see some changes, positive changes.

I recently phoned Umberto Rassi, then director of the General Conference Department of Education, and expressed some of my concerns, asking him if he ever took time out to dialogue with lay members.

He assured me that he did, indeed. "Go ahead and talk," he said.

"No, I'd prefer to make an appointment and come and talk to you face to face," I replied. We arranged a time.

I found him warm and attentive: "What are your concerns?" he asked. Then he listened to me for one hour, without interruption. "Are you finished?" he asked when I finally ran out of steam.

"Yes," I replied.

I knew he had listened, for in less than three minutes, he correctly summarized what I had just told him.

He told me he understood the issues I had presented and he explained that in the Seventh-day Adventist Church's decentralized administrative structure, the General Conference is unable to arbitrarily make changes in specific educational institutions. But unlike a host of his colleagues, he had listened carefully to what I had to say.

I hope leaders in all phases of Church administration will learn to do business this way—especially in our educational and Trust Services departments.

Chapter 3

TRUTH DECAY

Over Lemons
and Lemonade

"We want to avoid the appearance of promoting a certain area or project. The primary goal of the Trust Services representative is to determine what the person wants to do and to give the general information needed to accomplish those desires" "Trust Services: Colleague or Competitor?", *Ministry Magazine,* February 1991, by a former General Conference Trust Services director.

*R*eferences to some large sums of money will come up in chapters to follow, and I apologize. Not that large numbers are boring—a good storyteller has used them to spice up many a good who-done-it. What I apologize for is any appearance of display.

During the past 100 years, the Koppel family has made a lot of money—made it through hard work. And we've worked even harder (at times) to give it away! The Bible reminds us that our right hand should not know what our left hand is giving—that is, our giving should be cheerful and disinterested.

But in sharing my story, the record must include reference to these large sums of money. I know of no other way to tell this tearful story without telling it as it is. And the fact that the sums are large may suggest (as I believe) that business problems associated with handling large sums of money in the Church are significant.

Denominational attorneys, administrators, and clergymen are wordsmiths. Like artists on canvass, the best of them use abstract language to create incredible mental pictures. As a dentist, I tend to be more concrete. So, the word pictures that follow may not be artistically drawn, but they will be rigorously authentic.

When my father, Karl Koppel, came to the United States at age 23, his assets consisted of the $100 his mother had given him—plus $50 he had won in a lottery. Although Pop was fluent in German and Hungarian and knew some Serbian, he knew no English at all.

He was down to his last few dollars when a newspaper advertisement for a knitter on Staten Island caught his attention. To apply for the job, he took the subway to Manhattan's Battery Park, caught a ferry, and finally transferred to a streetcar. He applied for the job and was turned down.

The next week the same ad reappeared. And, being a tenacious man in tenuous economic circumstances, he applied again—and, again, was told "No." But the ad appeared a third time, a week later, and again Pop made the complicated trip. This time, the employer handed him a piece of knitting and asked, "Can you knit this?"

Pop examined the material and said, "Of course!"

He got the job.

Within six years, he had worked and saved enough to start his own knitting business, with 10 employees.

One Saturday, however, he consulted a fellow German knitter for technical advice and, instead, got a Bible study on Daniel 2 and the seventh-day Sabbath. Pop eventually joined the Brooklyn German Adventist Church, where he met and married Katharine Dontinville, whose parents had emigrated from Alsace Loraine. I was born on my parents' first anniversary, just two months after my mother's 21st birthday. But before I was born, Pop was drafted into the US Army as a private.

And it was at that point that Pop began to set a pattern of disinterested benevolence that remained until his death.

Days before he was inducted into the army, he donated his new Oldsmobile to his conference president. He had unquestioning confidence in Church leaders and developed a habit of almost compulsive philanthropy to his beloved Church.

It was also the beginning of years of interaction with Church leaders. Pop was a man of simple faith and an immigrant's need for respect, recognition, and approval. Denominational leaders knew this all too well.

When Pop went off to the army's Camp Upton in New York state, he left Mom to run the knitting business. Pregnant, she now had no automobile and had to make deliveries by streetcar. For months she struggled, carrying large bundles of children's knitwear all over the city to home-based embroiderers. Meanwhile, the conference president enjoyed Pop's new Olds, perhaps unaware of her hardships.

Even after Pop's discharge from the army, he was still struggling to learn English. But he quickly learned how to buy property at auction through delinquent real estate tax sales. He did well. In 1925 he picked up two farms, on the same day, for $10,000 each. Both were seven miles east of Trenton, New Jersey, in the small railroad town of Robbinsville.

One 70-acre farm separated Pop's two acreages, and in the early 1930s, at the depth of the Great Depression, its owner was unable to pay the $100 delinquent real estate taxes. Pop bought the taxes at auction and foreclosed, unifying his first two farms and bringing his total acreage to 200 (see map on page 114).

He learned to make bold moves in business and once bought $150,000 in delinquent taxes owed on the Robbinsville Airport, believing the owners might forfeit the property. When the owners finally came up with money to pay the taxes, Pop still made a tidy profit on the interest. He became an accomplished investor and did his best to pass those skills along to me, his firstborn son.

After buying the farms, Pop moved his knitting mill from Brooklyn to Robbinsville, on the main highway between Philadelphia and New York. At first, he set up the mill on the first floor of our old farmhouse, on the corner of Route 33 and the Robbinsville-Edinburgh Road; we lived on the second floor. The knitting machines ran by long belts, driven by powerful motors suspended from the first-floor ceiling. Once, when Mom was very sick, I remember her complaining about the noisy, vibrating motors that rattled her bed.

Pop's mill in New York had been located in an area where other German knitters plied their trade. So Pop knew nothing about farming when we moved to Robbinsville. But as in all his business ventures, he learned quickly by asking questions and focusing his time and energy on the challenges at hand.

How Pop was able to afford the many projects he started I will never understand. Money was scarce during the Great Depression, but he just kept moving forward!

He seemed unaware that making money was impossible during the 1930s—so he made money anyway. He expanded by building a new structure for the mill and dividing his enterprises into "Universal Farms" and "Universal Knitting Mills".

To cut construction costs on the new 110 x 55 foot building, he used timber cut from his own land and hired dozens of out-of-work laborers to hammer old cement from bricks salvaged from Trenton's torn-down porcelain factories. In the factory basement, he stored potatoes, while the mill occupied the main floor. The total construction cost for that key building came to less than $10,000; today, the building rents for $6,000 a month. Pop's Depression-era investment paid off handsomely.

Later, a local church member who built houses for a living told Pop he needed work for his employees and offered to build a house at cost—just to keep his workers busy. Pop took him up on the offer and for $8,000 became the owner of a home now valued at $165,000.

Of course, a few Depression-time projects did less well. I'll never forget driving a five-ton load of sweet corn to the New York produce market—and finding not a single buyer. We fed that whole load to the neighbor's pigs.

Pop's recipe for survival in hard times called for hard, hard work—and he led by example. I remember him down on his knees, weeding and suckering sweet corn from dawn to dusk. My brother and I each had a row on either side of him. To our left and right, five hired men did the same work. If we complained to Pop about the backbreaking labor, he would say, "If you don't keep up with me, they won't either."

He taught me the value of hard work—yes. But he also shared with me a sense of purpose and responsibility in financial matters.

He taught me the value of trust. For example, I always carried money—I had to, because I was always doing Pop's errands. When I'd return from an overnight trip to sell produce—primarily potatoes—in New York or Newark, I'd usually have a large roll of bills in my pocket.

After these trips, Pop would ask "What did you get per bag?" I'd tell him the price I'd received for each 100-lb. sack and would peel off a handful of bills and give it to him and put the rest in my pocket. He'd never count the money in my presence. He'd just accept my word.

I didn't think much about it then—about how much trust he showed me by treating me this way. But years later, it dawned on me how liberal he had been, and I asked him, "How did you arrive at that method of teaching us how to handle money?"

His answer, still inflected with that heavy German accent, was short and simple, "I was 30 years older than you were. I should know what I was doing." I consider that one of the highest compliments Pop ever gave me.

Pop was also a born philanthropist. His example taught me five main reasons why Christians should give:

1. To make it possible for others to know about God's wonderful gift of salvation;
2. To sustain the poor;
3. To show love for others;
4. To combat selfishness in our own characters;
5. To benefit one's heirs, in the spirit of the Old Testament patriarchs who gave "birthrights" and other substantial gifts to their offspring.

Pop was a progressive farmer and bought the first diesel caterpillar tractor ever used in New Jersey agriculture. The tractor pulled a four-bottom plow—another rarity of that time. When four-row cultivators came on the market, he immediately replaced his two-row units.

But staying on top of business, for Pop, was only a means to an end. He was always thinking ahead and looking for ways to benefit the Church. Years later, at age 75, he flew to North Carolina to buy at auction an 11-cubic-yard earth-moving machine. He had it trucked to New Jersey and spent $100,000, improving the topography of the farm.

"Why are you spending this kind of money and going to this kind of effort?" I asked him. I knew he intended to give the acreage to the Church.

"It will improve the value, and I can do it cheaper than the Church can," he explained.

For Pop, there was no "them and us" when it came to his beloved Church. He saw himself as a fund-raising, fund-sharing arm of the Church. He also lived the Adventist "health message" and prospered spiritually and physically. He loved working out of doors with his hands, in the fresh air, and at age 102 could still pull off a fairly graceful dive into a swimming pool. At age 105, his systolic blood pressure and cholesterol levels both measured in the miserly 120s.

But we live in an imperfect world of sin, and after Pop reached his 95th birthday, he began to become forgetful. And with that memory loss came frustration, suspicion, and even paranoia.

While visiting him one day, I noticed on his desk an unfamiliar name penciled on a pad. Could this be an attorney's name, I wondered, and indeed I found the name listed in the Yellow Pages under "lawyers."

So I drove the seven miles from Pop's home to the lawyer's office in Hightstown and joined six other clients in the attorney's waiting room. I gave the secretary my business card and told her I had no appointment, but was willing to wait. A few minutes later she ushered me into the lawyer's office.

"I know why you're here," he told me. "Your father thinks you're stealing his money. And when he came to see me, the first thing he did was try to convert me to his religion."

The lawyer shook his head and chuckled.

"I've checked up on you. You're okay," he said. "Oh, and by the way, before your father left he asked me how to get back to Robbinsville."

Pop had driven from Robbinsville to Hightstown and back hundreds of times and knew every street and building. But his sense of direction—along with his memory and judgment—were failing.

As I was reviewing one of his old federal income tax returns, a few weeks later, I saw that he had listed depreciation for a number of farm machines, trucks, and other equipment he'd never owned. I pointed this out to him, and he admitted that he could no longer keep track of all these details in his mind. So he asked me to look for a competent estate lawyer and gave me full power of attorney.

He was also going deaf, and for the most part I had to deal with the estate attorney myself. But I did my best to prepare my parents' Trust and Will in a way I knew they would want.

On advice of his attorney, for estate tax purposes he titled half his assets in his name, the other half in Mom's. Since I had power of attorney, one day I went to the bank to deposit $400,000 in treasury bills—half in each of their names. In the middle of the transaction, who should appear but Pop himself.

Though no longer able to see very well, he spotted me and shouted for all in the bank to hear: "You're stealing my money. I know what you're doing; you're putting it in Mama's name."

Though I knew Pop suffered some degree of paranoia, I was hurt and embarrassed. I excused myself and told the bank officer I would return later.

Back at the house, I reminded Pop that just the week before we had talked the matter through with an attorney. "I am simply following the attorney's instructions," I told him.

I don't know if he remembered or not, but he finally allowed me to return to the bank and complete the transaction.

Despite my then-101-year-old father's mental condition, however, Conference Trust officials during that time continued to press Pop to make complicated decisions on money matters—without consulting me or any other family member. And Pop's was not the only situation where this was occurring.

I'd once removed the impacted wisdom teeth of a General Conference official's 18-year-old daughter. Years later, when she was about 50 years old, she phoned me and told me she was now the care provider for both of her parents and wished to make an addition to her home.

"How can I help you?" I asked, genuinely puzzled.

Exasperated, she explained that she had first phoned the local conference's Trust Services officer, to talk to him about her plans for her parents' comfort in her home. Soon, two representatives arrived.

After that first meeting, however, the men told her they would no longer talk with her, but would only discuss the matter privately with her parents.

When the officers visited her parents, they seemed unmoved by the fact that her mother was sitting in her living room by her husband, stark naked.

"They seem unconcerned that my mother and father are totally dependent on me," she said. "Mom doesn't even bother to put on clothes, anymore, unless I do it for her myself."

Nonetheless, she told me that the Trust officers insisted on finalizing her parents' wills without her input and assistance. It didn't surprise me when she later told me that she could no longer belong to a Church that would treat its older members this way.

Another situation involved my longtime non-Adventist dental laboratory technician—a conscientious, competent German who worked with several of us Seventh-day Adventist dentists.

One day, he phoned me and said, "Al, I have a piece of property in Nassau that I have been unable to sell. Would your Church accept it as a contribution?" I told him I'd look into the matter and get back to him.

So I phoned the then-director of General Conference Trust Services and introduced him to my technician-friend. Soon arrangements for the gift were finalized.

Only later did I learn that no sooner had my friend made the offer to donate the land than a serious purchaser stepped forward. But because he had already contacted the Church, he kept his promise and contributed the land anyway.

I, myself, never heard another word on the matter from the Trust leaders. In the business world, a simple "thank you" for such help is routine. Personally, I was grateful that my technician had chosen to make this sizable gift to my Church, and I told his other Seventh-day Adventist dentist-clients what he had done. But from the Church I heard not one syllable of appreciation.

Such treatment is by no means confined to the East Coast. About that time, a survey was being done on the West Coast, assessing members' attitudes toward the Trust Services of their conferences.

When all was said and done, those who conducted the independent survey concluded: "The Trust Services of the Church are regarded as 'takers' rather than 'providers of service.' The Trust Services of the Church must work harder to earn title to the word 'service.' Until it does, many Adventists of means will remain reticent to contact Trust Services personnel as they make final plans for their financial future."

My mother, who was 11 years younger than Pop, told me specifically that the then-president of the New Jersey Conference had visited them after they had already contributed 165 acres and had suggested that they give the last additional 40 acres they owned.

During that same visit, he'd also said that if they wished to leave something to me (their heir) that the Conference would be glad to funnel that to me. Mom was concerned! Clearly, she felt this was evidence of an ongoing attempt by the Conference president to take advantage of Pop's declining mental condition to alter his long-stated plans for his estate.

This attempt by the then-president become even more apparent after Pop's death, in 1992, when I discovered a letter dated January 12, 1987, written by the then-president of the New Jersey Conference, drafted in Pop's name for him to sign. One of the effects of that letter was that about $800,000 of my then-101-year-old father's total gift of about $8-million to the conference should be designated for "administrative discretionary use."

Following are copies of letters he prepared in an apparent effort to get Pop to change the manner of distribution of gifts Pop had made several decades before.

January 12, 1987

Dear Elder_____:

Now that we have completed the deed to give my seventy, plus or minus, acre parcel of land to the New Jersey Conference, I wish at this time to indicate some of the special areas of work in New Jersey to which I desire the proceeds of this land , when it is sold, to be applied and dedicated.

As I have discussed with you some of the needs and plans of our conference. it is my desire that the funds be applied in the following manner:

35% as a perpetual endowment for Christian education at Garden State Academy to benefit students of New Jersey.

25% as a quasi-endowment for New Jersey evangelism.

15% as a fund for future expansion of the administrative facilities of the conference.

15% as a fund to be used in the new church planting expansion program in New Jersey.

10% to be used in areas of administrative discretion. (About $800,000).

This division of funds should thus help the several areas of need you discussed with me, and should help advance the work of God, and reach many souls with the gospel in our conference.

Please process the request with the New Jersey Conference Committee and Association. It is my prayer that God will use these resources, which He has provided, for the glory of God and the soon return of Jesus our Lord.

Sincerely yours,

Charles Koppel

Honestly, I am unable to understand why this administrator wanted these stipulations, unless he himself wanted the funds to be directed to projects he favored. The reason I say that is because I had been at the New Jersey Conference Board Room table when Pop finalized his gift to the New Jersey. At that time, Conference administrators asked Pop what he wished his funds to benefit. His answer, which certainly was different than mine would have been, was almost carte blanche —"You should know that better than I do!"

I wonder if Pop had any idea what "administrative discretionary use" actually meant. His mental and verbal skills were deteriorating, and toward the end, he became almost totally compliant with the suggestions of Church officials, and sadly (though they now deny it) I know they chose to exert influence accordingly. Among Pop's documents, after his death in 1992, I also found the following letter, dated the January 13th, and drafted in Pop's name by the same then-president of the Conference.

Dear Elder _____

I have indicated in a separate letter my desire regarding the use of the funds obtained when the land I have given to the conference is sold, and in this letter I wish to express my preferences for the use of the funds which will belong to the Trenton Church. It is my desire that this gift should become a blessing to the church by assisting the Church to expand and reach souls rather than to be absorbed in normal operating expenses and rob the members of the blessings of giving to the Lord for these expenses.

Consequently, I would wish that these funds should be dedicated in equal parts to local Christian education endowment, local evangelism, local capital improvements, and the final portion to local administrative discretionary use.

Please present this request to the Trenton Church Board, with the request that an official action be taken to distribute these funds in ways as suggested above so that my gift will have the strongest possible benefit for the growth of the Trenton Church. It is my earnest desire to see God's work proceed in the Trenton area....

Thank you.

Sincerely yours
Charles Koppel

One effect of this second letter was to redirect Pop's gift to benefit different causes than he had originally designated for the Trenton Church—Pop's and my home congregation.

These maneuvers on the part of the former New Jersey Conference President directly conflict with public statements of a General Conference Trust Services officer, who in a 1991 *Ministry Magazine* article cautioned that members should be allowed to designate what their contributions will benefit.

According to this former New Jersey Conference president, Pop himself suggested reducing the percentage to benefit the general fund of the Trenton Church. Yet, I have cited in these pages many evidences of Pop's senility during that period of time. Pop was often confused. Any fair judge could have ruled him mentally incompetent, during that time, based on his inability to answer the simple questions, "Who is the President of the United States?" or "What assets do you own?"

In fact, I had recently asked Pop to list his major assets. He couldn't. He admitted as much and said simply, "You know." Pop knew he was failing. But such was his faith in Conference leaders that it seems he allowed them to "guide" him in substantially reducing the benefit he had originally intended to give his local congregation. I believe this to be true, though the Conference now refuses to share the particulars of their verbal transactions with my then-100-year-old father. As further evidence of Pop's decline, at this very period of time he developed the desire to preach—something totally out of character for him. Yet, Conference administrators and/or local elders in smaller churches allowed him to do so at the 11 o'clock hour. My mother reported to me that on one occasion he got about five minutes into his presentation and had a "major senior moment." He just couldn't continue. They had the closing hymn and prayer and settled for a "short sermon" that Sabbath. I have no question that the Conference president had knowledge of these public evidences of my father's mental deterioration.

But let's look again at that second letter. The fifth designation states, once again, that 10 percent of Pop's estate be allotted for "administrative discretionary" use. If only the Seventh-day Adventist Church had a "Freedom of Information" provision, we could find out what was really going on when they prepared this letter for my father to sign!

Shortly after discovering this second letter, I perused the February 1991 issue of *Ministry Magazine*. There I read with great interest an article titled, "Trust Services: Colleague or Competitor?" The author is none other than the then-director of General Conference Trust Services—an attorney and ordained minister. He writes in that article of the need for gifts to go to local churches, as well as to conferences.

Addressing Church pastors, he writes: "Perhaps you have thought of Trust Services as working to direct your members' monies to the conference rather than to your church. You may even have heard of a Trust Services representative urging an individual not to leave anything to the local church. While such a situation may have existed in the past, I believe you will find that things have changed … to my knowledge all conference Trust Services programs now encourage church members to consider the needs of the local churches."

He continues: "We want members to know that they can leave to their local church whatever portion of their estate they wish.

"The primary goal of Trust Services representatives is to determine what the person wants to do and give the general information to accomplish those desires."

This General Conference officer makes things sound wonderful, indeed. But, given the kinds of experiences I've mentioned, and will share in later portions of this book, it's little wonder that he sadly admits toward the end of the article: "Our best estimate suggests that less than 10% of the membership in North America make any provision directing funds to the Lord's work."

After reading the article, I met with him and some of his staff at the General Conference and shared how the Conference had clearly applied pressure to my father, an ailing man, to change the provisions of his gift to leave more to the conference and less to the local church.

I told him that I understood the importance of confidentiality in some matters—especially if Pop had even once told them he wanted me to have no part in his financial planning. But he'd always trusted me and been very open on financial matters. In fact, when I was in the area, he always invited me to sit in on discussions with the Conference on matters of his estate.

I told them that as a contributor to the Church, I was vitally interested in the results of Pop's giving. Were his instructions regarding his gifts carried out as he directed?

I was met with chilly, stonewalled silence. Despite what the then-director of the General Conference Trust Department had written, it still appeared that no one was committed to holding Church administrators to minimal ethical standards or apologizing for clear cases of past misuse of influence.

I do not remember ever discussing with my parents what or how much of their estate they would leave to me. I felt they would treat me fairly. Not once did I complain that they were leaving too much to the Church. In fact, I assisted them by contacting various denominational officials involved with Church philanthropy. But I was disturbed when I learned that these officials had used their office to suggest to my parents how much to leave, or not leave, me. What shortsightedness! Don't they understand that today's beneficiaries will be tomorrow's givers?

Gary Smalley and John Trent, Ph.D., wrote a book titled *The Blessing* in which they say, "On the inside we all yearn for intimacy and affection. This yearning is especially true in our relationship with our parents. Gaining or missing out on parental approval has a tremendous effect on us.

Even if it has been years since we have had any regular contact with them. It fact, what happens in our relationship with our parents can greatly affect all our present and future relationships." Then they go on to describe the importance of an inheritance.

Abraham must have been aware of this, because Genesis 25:5, 6 says, "And Abraham gave all that he had unto Isaac. But unto the sons of his concubines, which Abraham had, Abraham gave gifts."

In the end, I received what I consider a very large inheritance and am sometimes surprised at myself for contributing most of what I inherited. When I meet my parents in the kingdom, I will be happy to give them my report card. Knowing that Pop went to his grave with total confidence that Church administrators would dot every "I" and cross every "T" of their promises to him, I can't help but picture what the scene will be when they render their report.

Some examples of member-exploitation by the Church may seem petty. But the very smallness often reveals an undercurrent of insensitivity to ethical standards in dealing with people like Pop, who hungered for the respect and approval of his Church leaders.

His desire to please Church leaders became especially pronounced during his later years, but its seeds were sown early in life. For example, I remember one Trenton Church pastor who seemed to live an incredibly disorganized life.

He would sometimes arrive two hours late to conduct weddings. And because our home was located on his route between the two churches he served, on Sabbath, he would not infrequently appear on our doorstep with an almost empty fuel tank. Pop would gladly fill up his car at the farm gas pump.

As Pop got along in years, I had no doubt that he would give most of his assets to the Church, so I asked him if he would like me to talk to the head of the General Conference

Trust Services Department. With his approval, I spoke with the then-director of the General Conference of Trust Services, who later visited my parents at their home.

Near the end of their first discussion, this Trust Services officer said he "understood" (a word frequently used by the brethren) that "the doctor [I] would like some of Pop's assets."

I was appalled when mother told me what he had said! I had never, ever raised the subject of my inheritance with Pop, this Trust officer, or anyone else. My only intent in contacting him had been to help Pop do what I knew Pop earnestly wanted to do—give sizeable gifts to the Church.

For the Trust officer to have raised the issue of an inheritance for me might have been readily forgivable, had he not gone on to counsel Pop that I really didn't need any of the family assets, because I had just sold my dental practice. Clearly, the General Conference Trust officer was exerting pressure on Pop to give nearly everything he had to the Church.

In later years, when I told a Columbia Union Conference Trust Services officer about this, he asked me if I had actually been present when these things were allegedly said. I conceded that I had not personally heard the remarks, but that my mother, who was there, had immediately brought them to my attention.

Later, I contacted this former General Conference Trust Services officer and asked him about what he had said to my parents. He admitted making these statements, but said he had added the disclaimer, "But, of course, that is up to you."

But even if he did add that disclaimer (one my mother does not recall hearing him use) it doesn't change the fact that this Conference official was urging an elderly church member to part with his assets, to the partial or total exclusion of his heirs. This is totally out of line with the claim made in the 1991 *Ministry* article: "The primary goal of Trust Services representatives is to determine what *the person wants to do.* (italics mine)."

In my experience, the "primary goal" of the Church's Trust Services representatives has been to urge Church members to give most—if not all—of their assets to the Church's general fund.

When the Columbia Union Conference Trust Services officer told me that some conference presidents had not yet bought into the new-and-improved Trust Services code of ethics, I was reminded that both he and the New Jersey Conference Trust officer, together in my presence, had told me "We do what our presidents tell us to do." The misadventures I describe in this book are by no means all hatched and executed by underlings. They permeate administration, and the greater the amount of money involved, it seems, the worse the departure from ethical standards.

How wonderful it would be if the Church could begin to live up to its stated goals! I've been encouraged by some recent statements in print, published by top Trust Services officers. But much work remains to be done.

In an apparent effort to alter these negative impressions, Trust Services is currently running full-page testimonial advertisements in publications such as the *Adventist Review* and *Columbia Union Visitor* and other union papers. Prominent individuals appearing in those ads and testifying to the virtues of Trust Services are undoubtedly sincere, but the facts as my family has lived them are far less reassuring.

This advertising blitz now includes television, and the present General Conference Trust Services director recently suggested over the air that contributors would indeed be pleased on resurrection morning to learn how much good their contributions had accomplished. Unfortunately, I believe my own father will be appalled when presented with the record of how his contributions fared under Church stewardship.

Chapter 4

TRUTH DECAY

*That Saved Pennies and
Squandered Millions*

"We want to emphasize the service aspect rather than just money" "Trust Services: Colleague or Competitor?", *Ministry Magazine,* February 1991, by a former General Conference director of Trust Services.

*T*aking large contributions is complicated business. The legal and tax consequences are significant and ramifications can be devilish and profound. Few donors study the tax code on their own. So most contributors are more or less uninformed about laws governing estate plans, philanthropy, and applicable tax law. Unfortunately, the same appears to be true of some of the Church's Trust officers.

You've noted by now that persistence was one of Pop's paramount propensities. That's how Pop got his first job in America; that's how we survived the Great Depression; that's how he made his millions. He was patient and persistent. He never gave up; he never stopped planning for success.

That persistent attitude has been the blessing—and the bane—of Pop's and my relationship with the Church. When we set our minds to do something, we press forward, and more often than not we succeed.

I'm convinced that most families that achieve wealth through enterprise and industry share this trait. It comes with the territory, and perhaps our Trust Services personnel should school themselves more thoroughly in the personality profiles of those blessed by God with strong entrepreneurial bootstraps.

I somehow expected that men of God who were interested in disposing of our millions would show the same, persistent dedication to detail we had invested in acquiring those millions. But in this I was profoundly disappointed.

So, as we studied out the most cost-effective ways to package his donations to the Church, Pop and I found it necessary to invest approximately $100,000 of our own money in legal fees—simply to educate ourselves on the true ramifications of the options set before us.

We are aware that Trust Services cannot give legal counsel. Much of our legal expense, however, would have been absolutely unnecessary, had we received competent advice and assistance from Church Trust officials. They could have told us that if we split our gift, we could save considerable money by achieving additional tax deductions.

But before moving forward, let me first itemize the assets Pop left to the Church and me (see map on page 114):

165 acres flat farmland—Donated to New Jersey Conference—Sold for about $8.25 million.

About 10 acres (of the 165)—Donated to Trenton Adventist Church.

Five acres—Pop gave me.

(I later donated these five acres to the New Jersey Conference [Worth $250,000 if sold with the 165 acres]. These instructions were made and a copy was sent to me. Were the instructions not filed? Were they lost? Or were they ignored? The New Jersey Conference has been unable to sell the five acres because they didn't follow Pop's written instructions to sell them with the leverage of the more valuable 165-acre piece. Instead, I was told that they offered this five-acre piece to Sharbell Development. Naturally, this large corporation was not interested in this rather insignificant bit of property—but *would* have purchased it in a package with the 165 acres.

This Pop knew. But the Conference officers neglected to follow written instructions and demonstrated clear lack of savvy in marketing techniques.)

Two acres containing my parents' home and a factory— Parents gave to me. It was valued for estate tax purposes at $290,000 when I inherited it. We wisely held onto it for 12 years; during that time its appraised value rose to between one and two million dollars. We then contributed it to the Loma Linda University School of Dentistry.

*Forty acres (with four-unit apartment building)—*Parents gave to me. I gave one half of the 40 acres, valued at $1.17 million, to various entities of the Columbia Union Conference. I gave one quarter of the remaining acres (valued at $600,000 when finally sold for $2.4 million) to Loma Linda University School of Dentistry and we retained one-quarter interest in the property.

The 165 Acres

Pop's property was very desirable. While he was living, he had at least three prospective purchasers contact him every week. Real estate agents would send him cleverly worded letters—written to suggest that he had somehow agreed to list the property with them. But Pop always caught them at their tricks.

Pop was smart in ways of the world, and while he loved to give money to worthy causes, he hated to spend it. For example, his old manual typewriter could type a straight line about as well as a drunk could pass a sobriety line after a Fourth of July beer fest. I begged Pop to allow me to buy him a new one. But Pop never permitted me to replace the typographical relic.

Instead, every time I visited him, Pop would ask me to type letters to several Realtors, denying that he had agreed to list his property with them. Time after time, his instructions were always the same: "We will never need a real estate agency when we sell this property." The steady stream of eager buyers made it clear that the moment we posted even the most elemental "For Sale" sign, we would be inundated with serious interest.

I also heard Pop give the same instructions to New Jersey Conference administrators. Their answer was invariably the same: "Yes, Brother Koppel."

What a surprise, then, when a man I had never met before offered me his condolences at my father's funeral—telling me that Pop had talked to him about the sale of his property, before he died. That raised a red flag for me.

Clearly, this Realtor intended to gain financially from the sale of Pop's property. Unfortunately, he eventually was able to manipulate the Conference and achieve that goal in a big way—siphoning off a $400,000 commission from the sale of Pop's 165 donated acres.

To have allowed such a travesty, the New Jersey Conference clearly ignored the instructions Pop had made through the years—that under no conditions should Realtors' commissions be paid for the sale of his donated property!

In fairness, Conference presidents and Trust Services officers are under no obligation whatever to agree to conditions imposed by a contributor. But once they give their oral or written assent, integrity demands that those commitments be honored. Such commitments can't be broken because the sellers "think" they can achieve a higher price. And they can't be negated by spreading the blame among several members of a committee. The former director of New Jersey Conference Trust Services (who chaired the committee that negotiated the sale of Pop's 165 acres) recently assured me that *"from the beginning"* (italics my own) he had honored Pop's wishes that the property not be listed for sale with a Realtor.

However, he went on to say that without the assistance of the aforementioned Realtor, the final sale price would have been $2 million less (I think he meant $2 million, minus the $400,000 realtors fee).

Pop knew that large developers work hand in glove with Realtors, who handle large commercial properties with a view to their mutual benefit.

I find it difficult to believe that this former New Jersey Conference Trust Services officer believes that the $50,000 per acre they accepted was maximum when Sharbell later sold some of those same acres for $500,000 per acre.

The fact that I was able to sell 40 adjacent (but far less desirable) acres for $60,000 per acre at approximately the same time demonstrates that Pop's land was marketed ineffectively, while unnecessarily forfeiting $400,000 in Realtors' fees.

The Realtor's appearance at Pop's funeral was his first step in a plan to accomplish what he wanted —collection of a large fee.

The failure was in the "Brethren" allowing themselves to be tempted by the apple (a supposed $2 million additional amount in the contract). There is no question whatsoever that had Pop's instructions to stay away from the clutches of a Realtor been followed, the eventual purchaser (Sharbell Development) would in time have paid the same amount, with or without the Realtor's fee. Sharbell Development was a well-known developer of land and was involved in the *Foxmore* development adjacent to Pop's 165 acres. It was no secret that Sharbell Development was vitally interested in the 165 acres. Had the Conference bided its time, Sharbell Development would have come to them with an offer—no question about it! But they chose to do things their way, against expressed instructions of my father and their promises to him.

The Realtor in question had represented himself to me as Pop's agent at Pop's funeral when he said, "I have been talking to your father." Now, however, it appears clear that his only relation was with the Conference. For several years, I had attempted to learn more from the Conference about what really happened—and had received different answers.

With the release of a preliminary edition of this book manuscript, I was finally able to "leverage out" what really happened—that the Conference had succumbed to the temptation of this Realtor in order to save themselves time and energy. I stand by my assertion that payment of the Realtor's fee would have been absolutely unnecessary, had the Conference been more savvy in its marketing and had it kept its promise to my father.

I am thankful, at last, to know who actually led out in the sale of the 165 acres—information that was withheld from me for several years. Amazing truths reveal themselves, at times, when secretive individuals face the prospect of exposure in a book of this kind. I have been literally working for years to assemble the precise data and interpretations I include in this book. If errors persist, I attribute them primarily to the mantle of secrecy that has kept me from uncovering each and every fact, in full. I abhor misinformation! To my knowledge, this book tells the truth, and nothing but the truth.

If the Conference could err so egregiously on the matter of the Real Estate commission, I can only imagine the other oral instructions they failed to record and include in Pop's file.

I know of at least one. At the north border of Pop's 165-acre property stood a one-room cinderblock house, on a one-eighth acre lot. An aged woman had lived there until her health required her to be moved to a nursing home.

But before she moved, Pop asked her about the status of her property, as he was interested in adding it to his large acreage. He learned that she was supported by the state and that the state would someday put her property on the market.

Pop believed the small piece of property was strategic

to improving the value of the acreage he had committed to the Church, and he told Conference administrators (in my presence) to track the property when it went on the market. "Yes, Brother Koppel," they dutifully replied.

The dirt on Pop's grave had hardly settled when a "For Sale" sign appeared on that small piece of property. Since the Conference now owned Pop's 165 acres that adjoined this small piece of ground, I told them about the "For Sale" sign and reminded them of their assurances. I was startled by their non-response: cold, stonewalled silence. They refused to admit to any recollection of their unwritten promise. They just would not talk.

It reminds me of an experience I had as a 10-year-old, when another boy and I were watching a carnival set-up in town. The Ferris wheel operator beckoned us and asked us to run several errands. In return, he promised to give us both a free Ferris wheel ride, that evening.

We ran the errands and that evening came back for our reward. But the operator pretended he didn't know us and shooed us away. We trudged home, dejected—our innocence defiled. For the first time in our young lives, we had learned how it feels to be deceived in the cold, cruel world.

And so it was with promises made regarding Pop's estate. Some years after Pop died, the 165 acres he gave to the New Jersey Conference were sold for about $8,250,000. Remembering the strange conversation I'd had with the Realtor at Pop's funeral, I asked the New Jersey Conference president if the Conference had paid a real estate commission on the sale.

Indeed they had, he admitted—$400,000.

He was not amused when I told him that if my father could know what he had done, he would turn over in his grave.

The failure to record or comply with verbal agreements challenges the Conference's credibility in the eyes of all Church members. It's no secret that the Trust Services program for ministries such as Three Angels' Broadcasting Network is growing at a brisk rate. And anecdotal evidence among retired Adventists suggests that more and more are leaving large parts, or their entire estates, to such organizations.

There's also anecdotal evidence that the North American Division of the General Conference is concerned by this shift of allegiance. Perhaps we will find that this challenge from independent ministries will help awaken the denomination to the terrible cost of its careless treatment of its parishioners' "trusts."

Pop, like many first-generation Church members of his day, believed preachers and administrators when they gave their word. After all, these were the men he heard from the pulpits calling for integrity, transparency, and forthrightness. Surely, the promises of such men would be ironclad, binding, and meticulously fulfilled!

But when Trust department personnel fail to honor their promises and commitments, they do their ministry great harm.

My response to these abuses is redemptive. In recording my experiences here, I'm driven by sadness, not spite. Not many families have invested as much as the Koppels have in the financial future of the Church. As my wife and I pass from the scene, we want *more*—not *fewer*— Church members to feel comfortable entrusting their God-given assets to our beloved Church.

But how can that happen when we see so many mistakes—so many variances from the line of ethical behavior among even our top Trust personnel?

In my dialogue with these men, I have been accused of misinterpretation, inaccuracy, and even truth decay itself (see Epilogue). But not one has been able to argue convincingly that I am incorrect in the overall thrust of what I have to say. I have been meticulous in my persistent efforts to ferret out the truth. And in some cases, the responses I've printed from these men add some interesting details to what I already knew. But none is able to convincingly refute the substance of what really happened.

After all, my wife, Betty, and I still owned one-quarter interest in 40 acres adjacent to Pop's 165 acres, which compelled the Columbia Union to include us in any negotiations regarding its sale. Our input, by the Columbia Union Conferences Trust Services officer's own admission, resulted in helping achieve a much better price—as much as $1 million more—than they would have done on their own.

My hope is that the Church will refine its efforts and work much more closely, and amicably, with families in the disposition of their relatives' property and assets. The death of a parent or close relative (I can tell you from experience) is a time of soul-searching and recommitment to the principles for which we stand. We need "servant leaders" who are willing and able to go the second and third miles in accomplishing exactly what the donor intended to provide for his Church and heirs.

When this happens, the settling of estates can be redemptive times of recommitment to the principles for which the donors lived. Contacts with family members— when made with forethought and Christian tact—can help reconcile family members to the Church and to one another, during their time of grief and transition.

Adventist Trust Services, however, still seems to favor treating heirs and relatives as threats to the Church's bottom line. This is indeed sad, because I would have given my eyeteeth to have been allowed to help maximize the proceeds of the sale of Pop's land. I had no personal interest at all in the situation—nothing to gain but the satisfaction of knowing that Pop's land had brought the highest return possible to the Church, just as he wanted.

Given the many irregularities in the treatment of my father by Church officials, especially in his final years, I would have had little trouble pursuing the matter in court. I don't think it would have been too hard to prove that the Church had overreached in its handling of my father's gift of land, and that the transaction be declared null and void.

That I did no such thing reflects my infinite regard for my father and his desire to give of his substance to the Church.

But the fact remains that tenacious litigation could have nullified that gift, had I pursued it—and some families do exactly that. The Church does well to worry about such things, because of its vulnerability.

The simple solution is for Trust officials to seek first to minister to donors and their survivors as souls for salvation, rather than sources of cash for the Conference. If Trust officials could get this straight in their minds, I believe the Church would have 100 donated and entrusted dollars where today it has only one.

Chapter 5

TRUTH DECAY

Regarding Giving to a Local Congregation

"We want the members to know the needs of the local church and that they can leave to it whatever portion of their estate they wish" "Trust Services: Colleague or Competitor?", *Ministry Magazine,* February 1991, by a former General Conference director of Trust Services.

*I*t was in the mid-1950s that Pop deeded the best 90 acres of his farm to the Church, but he reserved the right to farm it for life. He also stipulated that he wanted one third of the value of his gift to benefit the Trenton Adventist Church (later renamed the Robbinsville Adventist Church). The remaining two thirds were to benefit the New Jersey Conference.

These percentages were still in effect when, some 30 years later, Pop increased his gift of land from 90 to 165 acres.

At that time, a then-youthful Trust Services officer asked to speak with me privately one day, as we both were visiting my parents. We walked out to my car together, and there he expressed his concern that Conference administrators were manipulating Pop to sign documents Pop couldn't understand.

He then showed me three letters prepared in the Conference office—each written in advance, in Pop's name, and ready for Pop's signature. The first letter authorized reduction of the gift to the Trenton/Robbinsville Church from one third to 20 percent. The second reduced the gift to 15 percent, and the third cut it back to only 10 percent. I do not know if my ailing father signed any of those letters: the Conference refuses to tell us.

After Pop's death, Betty and I made a non-Revocable Unitrust and a Revocable Trust, while we considered making an additional Unitrust to benefit the Trenton/Robbinsville Church. Before doing so, however, we asked to know how effectively Pop's instructions had been fulfilled by the New Jersey Conference in the matter of his gift of land.

We were also monitoring how the Columbia Union was managing the $1.2 million entrusted to it. What we found was secrecy, non-answers, stonewalling, lack of information, and failure of Conference officials to show up at meetings they themselves had scheduled to supposedly discuss the situation.

Another interesting factor was the case of a second piece of Pop's property (mentioned last chapter in the list of land donated by our family). In his younger years, Pop had learned that the owner of a five-acre parcel of land that adjoined his 165 acres was in jail and unable to keep up his payments. So Pop had an attorney unravel the title, at a cost of about $1,000. Pop then titled the property in my name and paid the taxes.

When Pop finally got around to telling me that the land was legally mine, he explained that I should not sell it yet, but wait and allow it to be sold along with the adjoining acres he was donating to the Conference. That way, he assured me, it would bring a better price.

Years later, the then-president of the New Jersey Conference wrote the following two letters, one to Pop (with a copy to me) and the other to the New Jersey Conference Trust Services director.

We had the property appraised, and it was valued at $84,500. To get the best price, we all believed it would need to be "packaged" with the larger, 165-acre piece.

August 28, 1985

Attention
Trust Services Director

Please be advised Mr. Charles Koppel has requested that if the conference, at some time in the future, negotiates a sale for the Koppel [165-acre] property, provision be made for the sale of the small section of five acres, identified on the attached map, which belongs to his son, Albert Koppel, of New Market, Virginia, be included in the sale unless disposed of prior to the sale of the larger acreage. The proceeds of the Albert Koppel property are to go to Mr. Albert Koppel.

Thank you
XXXXXX X XXXXXXX
President

August 28, 1985

Mr. Charles Koppel
2343 Route 33
Robbinsville, New Jersey 08691

Dear Brother Koppel:

The enclosed letter is being attached to your property file in the Trust Service office of the New Jersey Conference to facilitate the sale of Albert's land with yours if at some time in the future the conference should negotiate a sale of these tracts of land. I am also sending a copy of the letter to Albert.

We trust that things are moving along smoothly in preparing the final paper work on your property. Feel free to call upon us for any assistance which we can give. Be assured of my prayers for God to continue to bless you and Mrs. Koppel with renewed strength and health and continued prosperity.

Heaven's best,

XXXXXX X XXXXXXX
President

In time, I donated this five-acre parcel to the New Jersey Conference, though in view of Pop's by-then poor hearing and forgetfulness, I doubt he was conscious of what I had done.

As I formally signed papers that day, donating this acreage to the Conference, the New Jersey Conference (former) president was with me in the Conference boardroom, along with the former New Jersey Conference Trust Services officer.

Though I do not recall the names of others present, I do remember that one of them was an officer of the Columbia Union Conference.

The brethren then asked me (I'm sure the then- president and Trust officer of the New Jersey Conference were still present): "Doctor, what do you wish done with the proceeds of this land, when it is sold?"

I told them I had memories of my mother-in-law, Isabelle Adams, of the Burlington, New Jersey, Church, baking, knitting, and sewing to help pay church expenses for her small congregation. So I told the men in the room that I wanted the Conference to invest the funds and give the income to the Burlington Church for expenses.

You would have thought I'd asked them to donate the money to a pool hall! They immediately began delivering short, three- and four-minute mini sermons, pointing out how foolish it would be to "take away from members the blessing of paying their own church expenses."

Clearly, they were trying to influence my decision— to get their way rather than to help me accomplish what I wanted to do for the Church. So, what to do? At that very moment, I remembered the advice I had received from a former General Conference Trust Services officer who told me how he had once paid his tithe by contributing appreciated real estate—thus avoiding capital gains taxes.

So I said, "Just put it all in for tithe."

Since they didn't seem to object to these new instructions, I concluded they would do exactly as told, though I felt they still weren't pleased with my choice. Surely, they would file a written record that the funds were designated as tithe.

But apparently no such record was made. Years rushed by, and the Adventist movement brought a succession of men through the offices of President, Treasurer, and/or Trust Services.

So, one day, I wrote a letter and asked the new Trust director a simple question—where were the funds from the sale of my donated five acres to go?

No response came, so being a persistent man, after several months I wrote again. Still, no response. Later, in a January 21, 2004, meeting in New Jersey, he told me that on April 1, 2002, he'd written to the Columbia Union Conference Trust Services officer and "asked for his advice of how to respond to your letter. I gave him all the information in my research."

What was going on? A short letter, indeed, could have answered my question. Either they

1. Had the answer in their records,
2. Had lost what was recorded, or
3. Had never recorded it.

Yet, as of three years later, I had yet to get a straight answer to my simple question: "According to your records, how will the proceeds of the sale of the five acres be used?"

It all reminds me of a situation in my office during the Donald Davenport default debacle in the early 1980s, while I was still practicing dentistry in the Washington, D.C., area. At that time, millions of dollars entrusted to the Church (and subsequently loaned by the Church to real estate developer Donald Davenport) were put in grave jeopardy, when Davenport was forced to file for bankruptcy.

During that sad time, the head of the General Conference Communication Department visited me for dental work. After sitting down in the dental chair, he asked, "Doctor, would you please close the door?"

Never before had a patient made such a request, but I did as he asked. After the door closed, he covered his face with his hands and began to weep.

"What seems to be the matter?" I asked.

"My phone is ringing off the hook with calls from the public, the press, and parishioners," he said. "They want to know all about the Davenport case."

"Well, why don't you save yourself a lot of grief and just tell them the truth?" I challenged. "Why is it so hard just to tell the truth?"

It seems to be terribly stressful for Church leaders to level with us. And the tendency to hold back, to stall for time, to try to stretch their wiggle room creates tremendous credibility problems, especially among observant members. I believe firmly that a scientific survey of current trustors in the denomination would show that a majority is lukewarm to downright ambivalent about the future of their money. Among trustors my age, the refrain comes through loud and dissonant: "We're giving our money to the Church, not because we're pleased with the Church, but because we can't think of a better place to put it!"

But the story of the five acres continues. In my trips from my retirement home in Virginia to New Jersey to care for my parents and their affairs, not once had I seen a "For Sale" sign on the five-acre property I had donated.

By then, the property had been in the family for at least 25 years, but no Conference official had ever contacted me regarding particulars I might have shared such as rights of way, selling options, possible buyers, and so forth.

So, 15 years after I'd donated the land, I wrote and asked both the New Jersey Conference president and the Trust department officer if the conference still owned the property. If it had sold, what price had it brought and what phase of the Lord's work had the money benefited?

Three months passed and I received no answer, so I wrote another letter. Still no answer! So I did what the Bible instructs us to do—I took another brother along with me, in this case the vice president of the Columbia Union Conference, and asked him to please encourage the New Jersey Conference to answer me.

He phoned them, and in a letter dated February 11, 2002, he wrote: "I have talked to the New Jersey Conference Trust officer, who will research his files and get back to you shortly."

I waited. Still no answer.

So I phoned the vice president again, and on March 21, 2002, he again wrote to the New Jersey Conference Trust Services officer: "Dr. Koppel has asked me to contact you about two concerns. One concern is that he has yet to get a response to his continued request regarding the status of the land that he gave to the New Jersey Conference several years ago. He has written you and I have called you. You informed me that you would look into this matter. You also referred me to [the New Jersey Conference President], without success. Would you *please* (his emphasis) respond to Dr. Koppel."

Still no answer, so I wrote two more letters, repeating my request for information.

Yes, some of these men had knowingly taken advantage of my aged father's mental condition and manipulated concessions from him in his advancing years. But the unmitigated failure on the part of the Church to dignify my repeated and earnest entreaties struck me as intransigence not seen "even among the Gentiles."

While engaged in this peculiar "Alice In Wonderland" experience, I read an article in the *Adventist Review*, authored by Roy Adams, associate editor. He noted how the United Way's credibility plummeted when its top executives were found to be drawing multimillion-dollar salaries, while contributors and volunteers made immense sacrifices to help others.

After reading the article, I wrote to Adams and suggested that the Adventist Church has its own credibility problems and briefly outlined the problems I was facing in dealing with Church leaders.

He replied, in turn, that he would do what he could to get me the information I had been asking for and would appeal on my behalf directly to the General Conference treasurer. I thanked him, but when months passed with absolutely no communication, I wrote him again.

He answered that he would need my written permission to apply for and receive the information I'd requested. So, I immediately sent him my permission. He wrote back that he had chatted with the General Conference treasurer, and that—small world that we live in—the treasurer remembered that I had removed his wisdom teeth when he was a teenager. The associate editor encouraged me to phone the treasurer at his home and shared his phone number.

When I phoned the treasurer, he told me that although the General Conference does control the functions of the conferences in accordance with provisions of the *Church Manual*, it does not "make" local conferences perform, nor does it control them directly.

Apparently the *Adventist Review* associate editor had been mistaken in believing the treasurer could press my case. But after some conversation, the treasurer did promise to bring up my issue with the New Jersey Conference president. I thanked him and asked that when he did, he allow me to join the conversation as a third party in a conference telephone call.

I heard nothing from the treasurer for a couple of months, so I wrote still another letter. A month later, he phoned me from an airport as he prepared to fly to Jakarta. He said he would be back in the United States within a month and would then arrange a phone conversation with the New Jersey Conference president.

Then he told me that he already had spoken with the New Jersey Conference president, when they had both attended an August 2003 Adventist-Laymen's Services and Industries (ASI) convention in Albuquerque, New Mexico. He and the New Jersey Conference president had spent about a half hour discussing my problem (I had asked that I be included in the conversation; this was not the first time this has happened to me). The treasurer reported to me that the Conference president had told him that he had delayed answering me because he thought I was talking about a different gift of property we had made to the New Jersey Conference.

The excuse was flimsy—in fact, preposterous. I had now written four letters and he had by now received both a phone call and a letter from the Union Conference Trust officer. Each communication had specifically identified a gift of five acres, made 17 years before. If he still had any question as to which gift of land I was referring to, why hadn't he asked me?

Patience gone and energy sapped, I finally contacted the tax collector's office and discovered that the New Jersey Conference still owned the five acres. So, that part of the question was answered. Then I learned that the New Jersey Conference president had promised the General Conference treasurer to get in touch with me to try to resolve the issue directly. To this day he has not contacted me.

The only face-to-face contact I have had with the New Jersey Conference president was on a trip I took to New Jersey for a scheduled meeting to attempt to solve the impasse. I attempted to make an appointment but was only able to work through his secretary. Finally, I went to the New Jersey Conference office without an appointment. His secretary permitted me to wait to see him, after he had finished his other duties. I decided it would be quite a while until he could see me, so I picked up a Bible and read through the 21 chapters of the Gospel of John (however long that takes), which was the subject of our Sabbath school lessons that quarter.

As I remember, my eventual conversation that day with the president lasted only about five minutes. The only subject we discussed was the disposition of the five acres we had contributed.

But I still did not have answers to several other questions. He did not attempt to resolve any other issues.

Later, I suggested to the *Adventist Review* associate editor that a Church able to minister to 13 million members surely should have the acumen to answer simple questions posed by one of its staunchest—and by now most longsuffering—benefactors.

Even an embryonic policy of openness and freedom of information should have allowed a competent secretary to answer my question within 48 hours. So I wrote another letter to the treasurer, only to receive a reply from his secretary, informing me that he was overseas, on another assignment. Apparently, he had forgotten to get in touch with me, as he had promised, but now I understood that he was relying on the promise the New Jersey Conference president had made to contact me. The treasurer's secretary assured me that he would phone me as soon as he returned.

But now, a third issue comes up—perhaps the crux of the problem. Pop knew that the five acres would bring far more, per acre, if they were leveraged with the sale of the adjoining 165 acres. Two letters from the former New Jersey Conference president to my father, myself, and the New Jersey Conference Trust officer clearly acknowledge his understanding of my father's thinking on that matter.

Pop made the stipulation because, in contributing large assets to the Church, he believed that we should help the Conference realize the highest returns possible—that old trait of persistence again rearing its head.

For example, during the sale of the approximately 40 acres (the residual of the 200 acres, after the 165 acres had been donated to the Church), another developer had offered $10,000 an acre more than Sharbell Development. Sharbell Development, in turn, had quickly outbid that offer. When I had suggested that the Church might well have raised the price of each of the other 165 acres by a similar amount and thereby increased its benefit by nearly $1.65 million, the Columbia Union Trust Services officer labeled my views "speculation."

Perhaps. Though I no longer lived in New Jersey, myself, not once did I visit Robbinsville without picking up valuable information that could have helped me market the property more effectively.

And I know of at least three letters—one to me, one to Pop, and one to the New Jersey Conference Trust Services officer—that clearly indicate that the troublesome five acres were to have been sold with the 165 acres, using the larger acreage as leverage.

I had been led to believe that the former New Jersey president was heavily involved in the pre-sale negotiations for the sale of the 165 acres. He, however, now denied doing so. Yet, he himself had written the letters (see various copies on these pages), explaining how the five acres were to be marketed along with the 165. Now, it appeared his instructions had either been lost, never recorded, or simply ignored.

The Conference was caught between a rock and a hard place. If it admitted that the five acres were not yet sold, they would be owning up to a serious breach of trust in not selling them, as promised, along with the much-larger acreage.

So, leadership apparently elected to stonewall—to drag out its response, year after year, hoping I'd just drop the issue. But I wouldn't, and couldn't. "It's not in my genes."

The last time I spoke with the New Jersey Conference Trust officer, he told me that the New Jersey Conference Committee had not yet decided what the funds from the sale of the five-acre property would benefit.

Of course, the decision is not theirs to make! The proceeds were earmarked as tithe at the time I gave the land. But now there seems to be no record of my intentions. Why?

I'm no conspiracy buff, and I'm not claiming that some sinister plot in Adventism is out to defraud donors of their legacies. Nor am I alleging that the Church is purposely playing fast and loose with donated assets.

What I am saying is that members deserve to know that

the funds they contribute go to the causes for which they are given. Children in Adventist kindergartens learn that a dime is worth 10 pennies, and one of those pennies belongs to God, as tithe.

Apparently at least some high Church officials missed this lesson, somewhere along the way. Tithe is apparently no longer a sacred, separate fund worth honoring.

But that's only part of the problem. By my calculations, their failure to sell the five acres with the 165 acres will amount to a loss of some $250,000.

But that's only the financial part. More important are the succession of unrecorded, unkept promises. Church members should know about such mistakes and incompetence. But, administrators still seem to believe they can skirt the accountability question and stonewall their way through. This factual account of my trials with the brethren is dedicated expressly to helping put those days behind us.

Why have my "servant leaders" refused, year after year, to communicate with me? Reason tells me that they believe the price for answering my questions truthfully would be too high—that it would unnecessarily confirm what too many already suspect.

These men may be incompetent, but they're not stupid. And when they hear that I'm "retired" and "86 years old," they feel safe filing my entreaties in File 13. If pressed, they can portray me as a man slipping down the slope of life.

We had a bit of a showdown on January 21, 2004, when I asked that the New Jersey Conference Trust Services officer bring with him and show me the records for the 5, 40, and 165 acres contributed by Pop and me. He showed up at the meeting—with no records. And he was still unable to answer my questions:

1. Why weren't the five acres sold with the 165?
2. What Conference fund stands to benefit from the sale of the five acres?

A friend of mine who has had similar problems dealing

with the Church told me, "Our Church has no means of self-cleansing, lacks meaningful discipline, and is devoid of real accountability. The natural result is that our Church has become saturated with compromised leaders who lack the moral courage to discipline one another."

James Londis was one of our favorite pastors during our 20 years as members of the Sligo Adventist Church, near Washington, D.C. Years later, I heard that he had taken up an unusual line of work, so I phoned him to find out what he was doing and was pleased that he remembered me. I asked him how he was spending his time, professionally, these days, and he told me he was serving as "Corporate Integrity Officer" of Kettering Memorial Hospital—a position mandated by the federal government.

I suggested that the Adventist Church needed just such an officer, too, but Londis responded that Church officials do not feel such a position is needed.

My experience with the Church leads me to concur with Londis' assessment. The Church sees no need to monitor or challenge its corporate integrity, past or present. Yet I know for sure that alert, informed lay members would welcome the establishment of just such an office for the Church.

At the time of my father's death in 1992, the two acres, improved by my parents' residence and the factory, were for tax purposes valued at $290,000.

But now, 12 years after Pop's death, this land had increased more than four times in value, to between one and two million dollars. The Robbinsville Church pastor had heard that we were considering making a contribution of this property to a worthy cause, and he pleaded with me to further assist his Church.

There was nothing I would have rather done. But when I considered the way the Conference had handled our family's contributions, I felt I could not reward that kind of treatment. I instead donated the entire value of this property to the Loma Linda University School of Dentistry.

The proceeds will provide dental services for the poor and subsidize mission dentistry.

Because we retained 25 percent ownership of the 40 acres and the apartment house, we retained some control of the sale of this property. This disturbed the then-director of the New-Jersey Conference Trust department. In an April 2002 letter to the New Jersey Conference president, he decried the fact that I was involved in the negotiations for the sale of the property.

But the history of these negotiations proves that not only was I benefited by being involved, but the New Jersey Conference itself received $10,000 per acre more than it had in the sale of the 165 adjacent acres. All told, the Columbia Union Conference Trust officer later affirmed that I was responsible for realizing an additional $1 million in income from this one sale!

I submit the following letter from Pop, written in his inimitable German-tinged English, as evidence that he shared my view:

Let me translate for you what I believe Pop was trying to tell me in that handwritten letter. He knew that 15 years earlier, a Hamilton Square farmer had sold his property for $50,000 an acre. Pop understood how rapidly land was appreciating in the area, especially land along major highways.

As a gifted dealer in property, he realized that the land was extremely desirable—as mentioned earlier, he was getting two or three offers on the land each week. He knew that buyers would literally stand in line, bidding the price up, when the land went on the market.

This very thing happened when we sold the 40 acres of land. We held the purchaser to the line and got $60,000 per acre (well above appraisal) for a parcel of land considerably less desirable than the 165 acres.

Then, we achieved additional thousands of dollars by negotiating for the buyer to pay all transfer taxes, rollback taxes, and avoiding a Realtor's commission—all for a savings to the Church of several hundred thousand dollars.

And, lest we forget, in the sale of the 165 acres, the New Jersey Conference paid a $400,000 Realtor's commission, plus half of the rollback taxes and transfer fee. We saved all of these expenses through my intervention in the sale of the 40 acres.

I have written elsewhere how Sharbell Development (the firm that bought both the 165- and 40-acre properties) inserted a Realtor's commission in the agreement of sale of the 40 acres.

But they promptly withdrew that provision when I wrote them the following one-sentence letter: "At no time have we ever authorized anyone to bring any asset we owned to anyone's table."

Through a trust, Pop had left me those 40 acres of property, with a four-unit apartment house. At his death, it was valued for estate tax purposes at $1,170,000. It was less than a year after I'd inherited this valuable asset that I contacted the then-director of the New Jersey Conference

Trust Department, and he made an appointment to meet me at the farm.

This brings up another concern: In the Church, things that should be open and freely shared are frequently kept secret, while things that should be confidential are broadcast far and wide.

The meeting at the farm began none too smoothly, when the Trust officer told me that he had already alerted the Columbia Union that I was preparing to give 40 acres of valuable property. What presumption! While it was indeed true that I had made the appointment to explore such a possibility, it was by no means a done deal. The reason I had asked him to meet me privately was to help avoid creating premature assumptions about my intentions.

I was well aware that the Union would eventually have to become involved, if things went well with our discussion that day. But this meeting was extremely preliminary—the Trust officer had completely overstepped his professional authority by announcing my supposed intentions to another office. I felt that my trust had been betrayed. If in conveying these feelings in this book, I offend this Trust officer, I apologize. Perhaps a story could shed some light on my negative feelings about such incidents.

Early in my practice, I considered a call to mission service in Valore, India. The call came after I'd walked four blocks to the General Conference offices to discuss the possible appointment with an individual whose name I no longer recall. When we'd finished our discussion, I'd said, "Please, don't say anything about this, because it could have an effect on my practice."

Yet, by the time I'd walked the four city blocks back to my office, word was out. When I entered my office, my receptionist blurted out, "I hear you are going to India!" Enough said.

But back to those pesky 40 acres of land. Despite the rocky start to my discussions with the Conference Trust representative, we did press forward with negotiation, preparing the necessary documents for the donation of this property. We were almost ready to sign when my attorney suggested that if we contributed the property all at once, we could not possibly take full advantage of available tax deductions.

So we instead prepared an irrevocable Unitrust for one half of the property and a Revocable Trust for the other half. At the time, my wife and I were living 300 miles from the property—in the Shenandoah Valley of Virginia. We realized it would be difficult to manage, maintain, and rent out the four-unit apartment complex from that distance.

But since the Conference would be beneficiaries of the gift of property, I proposed that the Conference consider managing the property—located just seven miles from its offices.

Many months later, in a letter dated April 2, 2002, the former director of New Jersey Trust Services wrote: "He (Albert Koppel) pressed the conference on the matter" (of the conference managing the property).

While it is true that I had delayed making a final decision on the matter for several months, at no time did I "press the conference on the matter."

On October 5, 1998, the Columbia Union Conference Trust Services wrote us, saying: "It has come to my attention that you have informed the New Jersey Conference that you have revoked your Revocable Trust in favor of setting up a trust with Loma Linda University. As of the date of this letter our office has not received a notice of revocation from you. If it is your intention to revoke the trust, please send us a letter revoking the same."

When I read that letter, I wondered why the New Jersey Conference would urge the Union Conference Trust Department to encourage us to hurry up and sign a revocation of our trust. After all, we were in our 80s. If we should die in a common accident, they would end up with more than $1 million more coming their way. Why should they rush us?

As I see it now, they must have believed that our letter of revocation would release them from their agreement to manage the factory and adjacent residence.

In a letter dated June 18, 2003, the attorney employed by the Columbia Union to manage the sale negotiations, listed the remaining balance to be paid on the 40-acre property, which had now more than doubled in value to $2,410,128. He also listed the distribution to be made as follows:

Loma Linda University Trustees	25%	$602,532.20
Columbia Union Conference Trustee	43.21171%	$1,041,457.87
Koppel Trusts	31.78829%	$766,138.74

When the Loma Linda University attorney received his copy of these calculations, he phoned me and asked me why Koppel Trusts was receiving 31.78829 percent of the proceeds, rather than 25 percent, as stated in an earlier document. This amounted to an overage of $168,138 to Koppel Trusts.

The Loma Linda attorney also questioned why, when the Columbia Union Conference owned 50 percent of the property, they received only 43.21171 percent of the total—shortchanging them $168,138.

His questions were good ones—some of the same questions we had been asking the Conference. But, again, our questions had been met with silence. And other matters about our trusts remained, likewise, unanswered.

Finally I consulted my own attorney. After reading our trust for five minutes, he told me that, according to his reading, we should have been receiving, during the previous 15 months, quarterly payments from the Columbia Union.

I wondered why, in all my discussions with the Columbia Union, I had not been dealt with forthrightly and openly. Why had I not been made aware of this delinquency? When, at a much later date, I asked the Columbia Union

Trust Services officer this question, he said that they were hoping that they could sell the property so that I would not have to be concerned about it.

That resulted in my having to spend about $7,000 to have our own attorney uncover the problem. It was embarrassing. Our attorney knew that I was a Seventh-day Adventist, and it was left to him to discover that the Church had been less than forthright with me. He also knew that I had attempted (unsuccessfully) to have the matter clarified by the Columbia Union.

In view of these difficulties, I felt it would be better if he—rather than I—spoke with the Columbia Union Conference Trust officer. When he phoned the Columbia Trust officer, the officer admitted: "Our attorney made a mistake . . . I had oversight over that, but I missed it. We both missed it."

He was undoubtedly telling the truth. After all, he wears the following official hats in the Columbia Union Conference:

Vice President
Public Affairs and Religious Liberty Secretary
Trust Services Officer
Secretary of the Legal Association.
Union Attorney

He "messed up," not because he is dishonest, but because he is distracted by his many competing responsibilities.

Consequently, the Union Conference Trust officer and the Columbia Union's outside attorney are responsible for the loss of $168,138 once designated for the Columbia Union Conference's various entities—all because an attorney made a mistake and the Union Conference Trust officer failed to catch it.

"I'm assuming you're going to tell everybody from now on that we lost the $168,138," he told me at a recent meeting. Why didn't I simply rectify the matter by "re-contributing" the money back to the Church? he asked. Then he accused me of being responsible for the loss of these funds because I would not re-contribute them.

After all I've been through, including the extra attorney's fees I've paid and the $24,000 in additional income tax we were required to pay because of the Conference's mistakes, I'm somehow disinclined to do so. Would you have re-contributed $168,138 if you had just experienced the following:

1. Years of less-than-forthright treatment by the New Jersey Conference, regarding five acres for which they did not follow instructions;
2. The loss of $400,000 because they paid an unnecessary real estate commission and did not follow Pop's instructions.
3. The refusal of the New Jersey Conference for several years (approved by the Columbia Union) to resolve the property management issue.
4. Our inability to have our case heard by a responsible, disinterested group.
5. A virtual slap in the face by the New Jersey Conference president, by not attending a meeting scheduled to hear our concerns, at a time set for his convenience and approved by him (related later in some detail.)
6. Their refusal to answer my questions regarding the purchase of the old lady's property from the state.
7. Management fee dispute brought up at Union Committee without inviting me to represent my side of the question.

How could I, in good conscience, re-contribute this money to an organization that treated its contributors so callously?

David McCullogh, in his award-wining biography of John Adams, the second president of the United States, quotes Adams as follows: "Liberty cannot be preserved without a general knowledge among the people . . . a right, an indisputable, unalienable, indefeasible divine right to the most dreaded and envied kind of knowledge. I mean of the *character and conduct of their rulers.*"

If that is appropriate in government, it certainly should be so in a Christian organization.

Let me share a suggestion from my days in the service. As a dental officer in the US Army, I learned that every officer has what is known as a "201 File". When we debarked ship in Bremerhaven, Germany, the commanding officer aboard gave me a letter of commendation for a job well done in managing a group of about 125 soldiers in one of the ship's compartments.

Later on during my two years in Germany, a Military Policeman stopped me and said, "Does the Captain know that he was speeding." He was very kind and respectful. A few weeks later my commanding officer called me into his office and talked to me about my speeding. That information also was placed in my "201 File." It is my opinion that both leaders and members would be well served by a filing system of this kind. Members from the most- to least-educated will make far better decisions if they have the proper information on which to base their decisions

But back to my negotiations with the Union Conference. In a letter dated July 10, 2003, the Union Trust officer wrote: "I received your letter of July 7th, 2003. I appreciated your clarification regarding the history of the management of this property. It has been a long and bumpy journey, but I believe a successful one. You were quite instrumental in helping us to get a good price for the property.

"Let me say again, we greatly appreciate your generosity to the Church. I recognize that you have not been happy with the way this matter has been handled, but I think in the end God is very pleased with your generosity."

It may be that God is pleased with our generosity, but I have wondered if God is pleased with how the Conference has handled things—including what I see as forfeiture of as much as $2 million in additional sales income, had they worked more cooperatively with the family during the land-sale process.

Chapter 6

TRUTH DECAY

Over Property Management

"Those of us who work for Trust Services want to be your allies" "Trust Services: Colleague or Competitor?", *Ministry Magazine*, February 1991, by a former General Conference director of Trust Services.

*T*he Union Trust officer wrote in a letter dated December 20, 1993: "Neither will the income of the Unitrust be reduced in any way as a consequence of the Conference's management of the property constituting assets of either of the Trusts."

At the closing of the sale of the 40 acres, the Columbia Union wanted to withhold $11,000 that the New Jersey Conference had paid to HOWCO Management Company, over several years. It appears that the New Jersey Conference president had decided that, because we had exercised our right to revoke a Revocable Trust, the New Jersey Conference would no longer be responsible for managing the farmland and apartments we had already donated to them.

So he engaged the services of HOWCO Management Co. to supply a service that other New Jersey Conference officers had agreed the Conference would provide.

It's interesting that the New Jersey Conference Trust Services officer (who later became president) did not allow HOWCO to deduct its management fees from the income of the apartments, as is the usual practice.

After five years passed, when the tax deductions had been used up, the property had more than doubled in value from $1.17 million to $2.4 million. Now, after having contributed one-half of the asset, we were in the same position as we were before: We had an asset worth more than double the value we'd started with.

At the closing of the sale of the 40 acres, somewhat more than $2,400,000 was received. Of this, the Columbia Union was supposed to get 50 percent, or about $1.2 million. But due to the Union Conference Trust officer's inattention to detail, this amount was reduced by about seven percent, to $1.04 million, cutting the Columbia Union Conference's portion from 50 percent to 43.21171 percent.

According to the stipulation of our trust, the $1.04 million was to be divided among various entities of the Columbia Union as follows:

50%	Robbinsville, N.J., Church	$520,728
16.67%	New Jersey Conference	$173,611
8.34%	Burlington, N.J., Church	$86,857
8.33%	New Market, Virginia, Church	$86,753
8.33%	Shenandoah Valley Academy	$86,753
4.17%	National Association SDA Dentists ...	$43,428
4.16 %	Loma Linda University Medical Center ...	$43,324
	TOTAL	$1,041,457

These are values as of the day they were computed. They could vary, up or down, depending on how they were invested.

It's worth noting, I believe, that the 16.67 percent, or $173,611, contributed to the New Jersey Conference quite handily covers the $11,000 in management fees they had been demanding from us.

Profit and Loss

I'm a dentist, not a land speculator. Over the years I have asked the Lord to give me wisdom and judgment in dealing with the large inheritance with which I was blessed— or saddled. It's been a huge responsibility and not always a pleasant one, when trying to give it away to the Church!

But it's reassuring to note that the value of the real assets we inherited, with the Lord's blessing, has doubled and in one case increased more than four times in value.

All in all, we have been blessed. At 86 years of age, we're still in reasonably good health. Though I earned a good living as a dentist, we did not become wealthy, so when we received our substantial inheritance, I had to learn fast. Would I squander my inheritance, as so many do? Thank God, He has blessed our investment strategies.

Now, the 40 acres had more than doubled, again, in value from $1.17 million to $2.4 million. We had to decide what to do with the other one-half asset in the trust. Given what I have told you about our relationship with the New Jersey Conference, we had no desire to give anything more to either that Conference or the Columbia Union.

In the 1950s, Pop and I had made a contribution of a couple of thousand dollars to the then-fledgling Loma Linda University School of Dentistry, and in 1959, I had closed my office for six months to serve for one semester as an instructor in the Department of Oral Surgery.

Even that far back, long before I had any idea of the substantial inheritance I would receive, I had begun asking questions of the then-comptroller of the College of Medical Evangelists, John Shull. I was interested in the modalities for giving. John was a good family friend, reared in my wife's childhood church in Burlington, N.J. Betty had been the five-year-old flower girl in his wedding, just before he and his bride embarked for mission service in China.

Given this background, I did what I had done at the beginning: I again gave one-quarter of the asset in a Unitrust to Loma Linda University School of Dentistry, intending later to contribute the last quarter, for which we have now made provision.

I can only wish that the New Jersey Conference Trust officers could have given us the quality of assistance we received from Loma Linda University. If only Trust officers could understand that helping contributors save money ultimately works to the Church's advantage.

One thing the Conference did learn came in the form of a letter of acknowledgement, April 2, 2002, in which the former New Jersey Conference Trust officer wrote: "Neither the Conference nor it's legal counsel realized the related personal benefit that Dr. Koppel's plan [of sale] would provide—the ability for him to be involved in the negotiations of sale of the property, the product of his 25 percent ownership."

My experience convinces me that Church administrators seem intuitively wary of informed lay involvement. I would suggest that, instead of his somewhat negative attitude about "the related personal benefit that Dr. Koppel's plan would provide (him)," he should have been singing "Praise God from Whom All Blessings Flow" that I had been able to be involved.

Truth be known, because of my involvement, the Church benefited to the tune of several additional hundreds of thousands of dollars—as I've explained earlier in this book.

Although I myself have never taken any courses in marketing, I am convinced that my father's business example and instruction helped me negotiate favorable terms in the sale of the 40 acres.

Had I been allowed some involvement—even as a consultant—in the sale of Pop's 165 acres, my knowledge of the history and particulars of that property could have helped the Conference achieve at least $2 million more from its sale.

As stated earlier, Pop had expected the land to bring up to $80,000 per acre. The Conference sold it for $50,000 an acre, less taxes and Realtor's expenses.

We did much better in our sale of the 40 adjacent acres— $60,000 per acre. The 40 acres was clearly less-desirable lowland that required the use of 10 24-cubic yard Caterpillar earth-moving machines to bring it up to highway level. All things considered, the Conference let the 165 acres "go for a song."

No wonder the Union Conference Trust officer later wrote me: "You were quite instrumental in helping us get a good price for the [40 acre] property." Case closed.

Another thing I was learning about my Church is the competitive spirit among conferences and institutions. I have yet to see a Church administrator rejoice that another entity of the Lord's vineyard has been blessed by the liberality of one of its saints.

For example, the former New Jersey Conference Trust officer wrote to the New Jersey Conference president on April 2, 2002, saying: "During those negotiations I also learned that prior to contacting the New Jersey Conference, Dr. Koppel had approached both Loma Linda University and the Potomac Conference about funding a gift annuity with his New Jersey property. Both organizations apparently turned him down, primarily because of the impracticality of long-distance management of the gift property, and perhaps the pitfalls of funding an annuity with real property."

Not true. I had indeed asked a lot of questions of various institutional leaders, through the years, including the Potomac Conference and Loma Linda University. But at no time had I ever asked them about funding a gift annuity with our property. They did not turn us down for the simple reason that we never offered either of them the property!

Chapter 7

TRUTH DECAY

*Regarding a $11,000
Management Fee*

"Those of us who work for Trust Services want to be your allies" "Trust Services: Colleague or Competitor?", *Ministry Magazine*, February 1991, by a former General Conference director of Trust Services.

On December 21, 1993, the former New Jersey Conference Trust officer wrote: "I hope you will enjoy the freedom you now have after being relieved of the management responsibilities of your apartments and farmland."

What a wonderful sentiment! But complications had only just begun.

We fully believed our lives would indeed be less complicated, but what was our surprise a few years later when the then-director of New Jersey Conference Trust Services asked us to resume management of the very property they had agreed to manage a few years before, as noted in a letter from his predecessor, "Robert Boggess, Dowel Chow, and I agreed that the Conference would manage the four unit apartment building *until the property was sold.*" (emphasis mine)

Clear Agreement

These three had planned to manage the property in-house, since the property was only seven miles from the New Jersey Conference office. The agreement to manage the property was made on the basis of an irrevocable Unitrust for half of the property and a Revocable Trust for the other half. The former New Jersey Trust Services officer and Conference officials knew exactly what they were agreeing to.

If, during the existence of those trusts, my wife and I were to die, they knew that the Conference would be the recipient of the total value of both trusts, which at that time were valued at $1.17 million. They also knew that we had the right to revoke the Revocable Trust.

No Record

Though this correspondence clearly stated the terms, apparently no record of the promise to manage the property was ever recorded. So, the next Conference Trust Services director found it necessary to search out one of the three, who was by then living in Illinois, to determine the accuracy of my contention that such a commitment had indeed been made. In his letter of response to the New Jersey Trust officer, his predecessor admitted that my position was correct.

But since the then-director of New Jersey Trust Services had no documentation of the agreement, he came to me and suggested he was too busy maintaining the residences of pastors and wished to discontinue managing our apartment complex and that I resume the responsibility.

I told him this was out of the question, because one of the reasons we'd made the trust agreement in the first place was that we no longer wanted to manage the property.

I was learning how conferences work!

Things Get Worse

But things only got worse. After I told the New Jersey Conference Trust officer we were not in a position to manager the property (we were living 300 miles away!), we heard little more about it for five years. Then came a written demand that we pay a debt of $11,000, which the Conference had incurred by hiring a property management company.

We were not responsible for this debt—a debt quite trivial, I might add, when compared with the more than $1 million we had given.

But the Conference wouldn't drop the matter and applied psychological pressure for us to pay up. In a letter dated February 3, 2004, the Columbia Union Conference Trust Services officer wrote, "I also want to address your rationale for your position. You say your position is a matter of principle. The funds used to pay HOWCO were funds that came out of the general funds of the New Jersey Conference. The source of those funds were the constituents from all over the Conference. By not reimbursing the Conference, you are asking all of the 11,000 constituents to fund *Your Unitrust*. That is not only illegal but just not right. Don't you agree that would be a misuse of Church funds? . . . I would hope that you would not let the work of God in New Jersey suffer because of what you call principle . . . Please be assured that if you do not agree, I am obligated to go to court and I believe we will win."

I could not believe the short-sightedness of the Columbia Union Conference, threatening a contributor of more than $1 million in order to obtain a net additional return of less than one percent!

What was going on! We had given land valued at more than a million dollars—land that was rapidly appreciating. In our trust we had contributed much more than $100,000 to the New Jersey Conference (all the Conference Constituents). That amount would easily pay the $11,000 they were demanding. And the New Jersey Conference was now prepared to take us to court because I would not pay to have it managed for them! Was I dreaming?

No, that couldn't be. So I decided to go to my files and carefully review an eight-inch stack of letters regarding the trust property. It took quite a bit of time, but I finally came to a letter dated June 30, 1999, addressed to me, from the then-New Jersey Conference Trust director. In that letter he writes: "On July 1st we will turn the management of the apartments over to . . . HOWCO Management Company. As previously agreed, you will not personally be liable for any of these costs. The New Jersey Conference is bearing this responsibility."

How much plainer could it be? I sent a copy of the letter to the Union Trust director, and he later phoned me and said that in light of the 1999 letter, he now saw things my way. Hallelujah!

But let's look at some of the earlier reasoning of these "servant leaders." The Columbia Union Conference Trust officer, speaking as an attorney in his February 3, 2004, letter, says it is both wrong and illegal for me to ask the Conference to fund my Unitrust "from the monies contributed by all the constituents of the New Jersey Conference."

If this were indeed the case, why wasn't it wrong and illegal to do so back in 1999, when the New Jersey Conference president sent me that letter? Furthermore, I later learned that the Union Conference Trust officer, who also is an attorney, had specifically approved the provisions of the 1999 letter.

This whole incident—laughable as it may be to some—comes down to a question of professionalism and ethics. Just before Pop died, leaders were willing to allow Pop, in his senility, to make changes in the provisions of his gift—changes that ran counter to some of his clearly stated intentions of decades before.

Perhaps, now, they believed that as I reached my mid-80s, I had begun to soften mentally, physically, and strategically. Our Trust leaders may at times be incompetent, but they are not stupid. They know that the great equalizer in their calculations is time—as members age, they can be led to make commitments they might not have made at the height of their mental and physical powers.

This needs to change! The Church cannot afford to be seen as pressuring the infirm and afflicted. Integrity demands that we come to terms with the questionable behavior of our past and take steps to change it.

TRUTH DECAY

Regarding a Missed Meeting of Minds—
January 21, 2004, News Jersey Meeting

*A*fter several years without an answer to our simple questions regarding the five acres (Had they been sold? If so to whom? And how had the funds been disbursed?), the Union Trust officer was finally able to arrange a meeting. He made it at a time convenient to, and selected by, the New Jersey Conference president.

I suggested that we would need about three hours for the meeting. I had attended many meetings in the New Jersey Conference boardroom when dealing with Pop's and my contributions and had seen how the Conference president was often interrupted. This time I wanted his full attention. So I suggested to the Union Trust director that the meeting be held in the new Robbinsville Church, only about six miles from the Conference office.

I rescheduled some surgery I had planned and made plane and motel reservations. The only flight on the day of the meeting would have gotten me in a little late, so I booked a flight for the day before.

When I arrived in New Jersey the day before the meeting, the New Jersey Conference president's secretary phoned me on my cell phone and informed me that the meeting place had been changed and would now convene in the Conference office. She added that the president had scheduled a separate all-day meeting (right over the time of the scheduled meeting) that would take priority on his schedule.

I told the secretary that the new arrangement was

not satisfactory. I had not set the time and I understood it had been set to suit the New Jersey Conference president. Since the meeting involved several individuals in addition to myself and the president, I did not feel I had authority to agree to the change.

At the appointment time—10 a.m.—four of us were present, none from the Conference. The New Jersey Conference Trust officer arrived on schedule, but remained in his car until the Union Conference Trust officer arrived at 10:30—late, he explained, due to traffic problems.

The New Jersey Conference president himself never showed up, and I was frankly embarrassed that day to call myself a Seventh-day Adventist. How sad to see professional gospel ministers feinting and dodging the opportunity to solve problems together.

Kenneth Wood, former editor of the *Review & Herald* (now *Adventist Review*), had written me a letter in July 2001, warning me of the treatment I could expect from the "brethren."

Commenting on the stonewalling propensities of Adventist leaders, he said, "I have had the same kind of experience many times throughout the years. These experiences are not only wrong in themselves, they damage one's personhood. By being given the impression that one is not even worthy of a reply, they diminish one's feelings about himself."

It all reminds me of the preface to 2 Corinthians in the *New Message Bible*: "For anyone operating under the naïve presumption that joining a Christian church is a good way to meet all the best people and cultivate smooth social relations, a reading of Paul's Corinthians correspondence is the prescribed cure.

"Because leadership is necessarily an exercise of authority, it easily shifts into an exercise of power. But the minute it does that, it begins to inflict damage on both the leader and the led."

By now, I had invested five days' time and $1,000, trying to meet with the brethren and resolve my concerns. Here I was, on their doorstep, and the man I most wanted to see failed the appointment which had been made for his convenience.

So, our meeting that day began 30 minutes late—without the president. What concerned me most was that I was being heard by only two Conference leaders—both of whom had contributed directly to my grievances. Could they—would they—be able to objectively consider my concerns?

Addressing these two Church leaders (The Union and New Jersey Conference Trust officers), I said, "I find it impossible to believe that you servant leaders have refused for several years to communicate with me. I have wracked my brain. I can't come up with a reason why you have treated me this way.

"I disagree with a few people in this world, but never so much that I won't speak with them. I am a sinner and the Lord loves me. Everyone else is a sinner, and God loves them. What right would I have to cut off communication with anyone whom God loves? If I were to refuse to talk with any of God's children, I would feel unworthy to partake in the next ordinance of humility."

In response, the Columbia Union Trust officer suggested that the Koppels had been more difficult to deal with than other contributors. As evidence, he pointed out that, compared to his 15 other trust holders, our trust required the most correspondence space.

In turn, I couldn't help reflecting that ours was the only trust of the 15 whose assets were real estate—and may well have been the largest in monetary value. It also contained reams of pages having to do with an environmental problem related to the property.

Our file also included about 17 revisions of an approximately 40-page "Agreement of Sale" document. Complex? Yes. Difficult? Maybe.

Frankly, I believe a lot of the problems regarding our land and its sale are attributable directly to the many additional responsibilities the Union Trust officer has to carry—the many hats he wears—at the Columbia Union Conference. His attention is divided, his concentration scattered. These are facts with which he agrees.

Our voluminous file, in fact, included many three-page-letter "nudges" from me and the Union Conference's own attorney. This needling was needed, from time to time, to move the Union Trust officer to action.

During our meeting, I also brought up other issues. I noted that the Columbia Union offices are open only four days a week—understandable in a Church where pastor-administrators frequently preach on Sabbaths and attend meetings on weekends and evenings. But the limited number of office days does make it more difficult for people in the business community to interact with conference officials regarding matters of trade and finance.

Furthermore, I noted, Union officers frequently travel to attend committee meetings in far-off places. I have found them to be in Hawaii, Italy, Bermuda, Africa, and even India.

When I phoned, I would often get a recorded message, "I am away from my desk." Such a message tells me very little. Is the person down the hall in the lavatory, or on business in Africa? Good servant leadership calls for better accessibility and openness.

In the meeting, I also brought up the issue of the legality of some of the Church's investment practices.

When I'd spoken to the Loma Linda University attorney about our trust with the Columbia Union Conference, he noticed that the following amounts were invested in denominational funds: $66,809 invested in Columbia Union Revolving Fund and $225,000 in the General Conference Income Fund.

The attorney immediately told me that, in his opinion,

such investments could be considered "Self Dealing" on the part of the Columbia Union, and therefore illegal by Internal Revenue Service standards.

Concerned, I carefully re-read the text of our trust agreement and found that those exact words, "Self Dealing", appeared just as the attorney anticipated they would.

When, in good faith, I mentioned this to the Union Conference Trust officer at the New Jersey meeting, he seemed irate and said I was denigrating these two denominational investment vehicles.

He missed the point. I have nothing against these two funds and have independently invested in one of them several times—in one case more than $100,000. I would never invest that kind of money in funds I did not trust.

My whole point in raising the issue was to determine if the Union—and hence my trust—were on solid, legal ground by IRS standards. Frankly, I told him, it would be more appropriate for him to check the matter out discreetly rather than for me to raise it personally with the IRS and be seen as a whistleblower—a troublemaker for the Church. I still have not received an answer to my question!

At the meeting, I also brought up the matter of not having received an answer to our inquiry as to where the Conference record showed the proceeds from the sale of the five acres would be used.

To my amazement, the Union Conference Trust officer responded: "You gave it, so forget it." Excuse me? Last I checked, contributors to the Seventh-day Adventist Church have the right to designate how they want their contributions used.

Clearly, we were going nowhere in the meeting. Every point I raised, it seemed, brought irritated responses from my servant leaders. How could we ever resolve these issues, if we could not discuss them openly and without defensive rancor?

Perhaps the day will come when all of our conferences

set up mediation commissions as permanent parts of their governance. The Southeastern California Conference Executive Committee seems to be leading the way. It's long overdue.

As things stand today, I'm reminded of a time when our daughters were between four and six years of age and we were motoring together in Florida. A small-town policeman stopped me for exceeding the speed limit in a school zone. As the officer approached the car, I lowered the driver's side window. "Where the h__ do you think you are going?" he challenged, adding a long list of profanities. When he came up for breath, I said, "Officer, if I have broken the law, I am willing to pay the appropriate fine. You are a public servant. I do not use that kind of language, and I do not appreciate your using that kind of language in front of my children."

He sent me on my way: "Get out of here!"

No, our Conference officials don't use profanity. But they're not above posturing, intimidating, and shifting issues on those who challenge them—just like that small-town Florida cop. When they resort to these tactics, it cheapens our Church and perpetuates the cycle of distrust that alienates so many Adventists.

I recently enjoyed watching a televised discussion of the Sabbath school lesson, moderated by Pastor Doug Batchelor in the Sacramento Central Church. The title of the lesson was "Supporting Our Leaders." I was surprised when Batchelor suddenly asked any in the audience to raise their hands if they had experienced problems with leaders. What appeared to be about 80 percent of the audience raised its hands!

If I were a Church leader and had that many members having problems with their leaders, I would be concerned.

Back in the days when I was practicing dentistry, once or twice a year we would include with our patients' statements a self-addressed, postage-paid, anonymous questionnaire. Patients could complain or compliment us, as they chose.

We never received more than a one-percent return. Had there been an 80 percent negative return, I would have been so discouraged I would have left town.

Even today, my wife and I frequently receive such forms from businesses, hospitals, and professional offices. Considering the evidence of disaffection with Church leaders, the Church would be wise to initiate such surveys. Why shouldn't a Christian institution study how to do better?

Several months ago, I picked up an issue of the *Columbia Union Visitor* and read with interest the Columbia Union Conference president's goals for the following year:

To assure quality.

To survey constituents' needs and attitudes.

To connect with every member.

To listen to members' needs and views.

To facilitate more effective communication.

To mobilize the financial resources of every member.

To demonstrate good stewardship, and

To report how tithes and offerings are used.

In my experience, few of these goals are in imminent danger of being met! The Church seems absolutely incapable of rising to anything close to these standards. But I wish the brethren well.

But back to the aftermath of the January 2004 meeting. Granted, only two Conference officials were present, with no executive presence to help break impasses. If the New Jersey Conference president's absence had been a simple matter of inadvertent double scheduling, he could have called on another administrator—or perhaps a retired leader— to carry his message and help hammer out a memo of understanding.

But no, in effect he sabotaged the meeting through his deliberate and unapologetic absence. It was the final straw. It was time to go public with my concerns—to ask the whole Church to "help me reach these men who refuse to sit down with me and work out our differences."

What more can I do that hasn't been done? Where else could I turn, when the General Conference treasurer himself and the Columbia Union Conference Trust Services officer seemed unable to help me arrange a productive meeting?

During our meeting, The Union Trust officer tried to defend the Conference president, suggesting that some conference presidents had not yet bought into the new-and-improved Trust Services goals articulated 13 years before by the then-director of General Conference Trust Services in his *Ministry* article, "Trust Services: Colleague or Competitor?"

Yet, it's clear from my dealings that Conference Trust Services officers are usually beholden to the judgment of conference presidents—the two Trust officers present at New Jersey meeting acknowledged as much.

At one point in that meeting, I pressed the New Jersey Trust officer on why he had not answered my simple inquiries about what fund—or ministry—would benefit from the sale of the five acres.

He replied that he had to defer to his Union and local Conference superiors (one of whom was present) for answers. That struck me as odd. Clearly he feared repercussions if he gave me an honest answer, on his own; so he threw the hot potato to his superiors—one of whom conveniently was not there.

How sad that our January 21, 2004, meeting failed completely. Finally, the matter was scheduled for consideration at a Columbia Union Conference Board Meeting. The New Jersey Conference president attended, as an ex officio board member, and presented his view of the problem. Though I had repeatedly asked to be heard, I was not invited to the meeting.

Have these man no shame?

Chapter 9

TRUTH DECAY

Concerning the
Privileges of Membership

"Adventists are not generally known for being easily led by others. Those who have been in the church for many years know exactly where they want their money to go" "Trust Services: Colleague or Competitor?", *Ministry,* February 1991, by a former General Conference director of Trust Services.

*I*n the book *Questions on Doctrines,* page 97, Ellen G. White is quoted as mentioning certain "benefits and privileges" of membership in the Seventh-day Adventist Church.

In these final chapters, I challenge our Church to write and ratify a list of these "Benefits and Privileges"— in essence, a "Bill of Rights" for Adventist members.

I have searched the Seventh-day Adventist *Church Manual,* which lists a great deal of information about the function of the Church, but have been unable to locate any such list.

And when I wrote the Biblical Research Institute of the General Conference of Seventh-day Adventists, asking if they could locate a list of "benefits and privileges of Church membership," they said, "No such list exists."

When I brought the same question to the Union Trust officer, he said, "I don't know that the Church is designed to give benefits to members," and, "I don't know what benefits there are."

I don't either! And I wish I did.

My quest for this elusive list of "Benefits and Privileges" began during my nerve-wracking quest for answers about the five acres of property I had given the Church.

A Seventh-day Adventist should be able to donate for designated projects and find out where the money actually goes. He should be guaranteed speedy responses to questions of legitimate concern. On private matters, he should have absolute guarantees of confidentiality. And when disputes arise, he should have guaranteed access to an impartial court of appeal.

Perhaps because of our doctrinal emphasis on the shortness of time, we never imagined we would need to think through the issue of members' benefits and privileges. In an ideal world, we would all be so busy proclaiming the gospel, we wouldn't have time for disputes, appeals, or mediation.

Yet, the history of the Church is rife with accounts of damaging disputes—so much so that several decades back, the General Conference voted to ask members not to sue one another—or the Church for that matter—in courts of law. But it left woefully unanswered the question of how and where those with disputes could find the kind of unbiased, informed mediation necessary—especially in questions involving the policy or practice of Church officers themselves.

The Executive Branch of the Church—from local conference to General Conference committees—is intricately interwoven in an almost seamless fabric of networking individuals. To expect these Church employees to leave their executive credentials at the door and become, even for a few hours, an impartial judiciary, mediating a dispute between Albert Koppel and the New Jersey Conference, is wishful thinking.

Adventism must provide among its benefits and privileges access to a legitimate body with the credibility and knowledge necessary to mediate even complex financial questions (with impartial, expert help called in from time to time to help sort out especially difficult questions).

We now live in a so-called "postmodern era," where relationships are seen as more important than technology.

"Postmodernism," like it or not, places great value on unity and social cohesion, as indicators of corporate health. What better way to serve our younger members than to invent, with their input and insight, a system of mediation that respects the benefits and privileges we view as "inalienable" to membership in the Adventist Church!

Recent Sabbath school lessons have emphasized the importance of relationships. It's about time!

TRUTH DECAY

Final Thoughts on
Service and Accountability

*A*llow me to explain some simple facts about giving. When a donor contributes to a charitable institution in the form of a "Type 2 Unitrust", the donor is promised a set percentage of annual return on the gift. Suppose someone gives $1 million to the Church and is promised a rate of 8 percent annual return (if earned). The donor, then, can expect to receive from the Church $80,000 a year, until death.

The percentage of return is usually dependent on the donor's age when he makes the gift. The older the person, the higher the rate of promised return. A contribution of land generally provides the donor little or no return, until the land is converted to cash—in other words, sold.

A "Type 1 Unitrust" allows the charitable organization to accept funds and pay the trustor a set percentage—say, eight percent—whether the fund earns that amount or not. If it is not earned, whatever amount of the payment that exceeds the earned amount is taken from the principal of the trust.

Our Unitrust with the New Jersey Conference was funded mostly with land, and for approximately 10 years we received relatively little income. The real estate was sold in 2003—converting our trust assets to cash.

Most Trust donors take advantage of the Type 1 Unitrust. But there's an important advantage to donors, like Pop and me, who gave real estate assets, in that capital gains taxes can be avoided in this way, offering substantial savings to both the donors and the Church.

After our unfortunate recent experiences with the New Jersey Conference, my wife and I signed a Unitrust with Loma Linda University, funded with land. When we elected to flip (convert our Unitrust to a Type 1 Unitrust), Loma Linda University's attorney did the legal work at no charge—the same as he did for approximately 150 other trusts.

On the other hand, when we asked the Columbia Union Conference to flip our trust, they employed an outside attorney and charged us $3,667 for the work. At the same time, the outside attorney also flipped the 15 other trusts the Columbia Union Conference officer said they held. Each of these trusts was charged the same fee—earning the attorney about $58,000, total. If his fee was $300 per hour, he must have worked for almost 200 hours—about five full weeks— on this project alone!

I told the Columbia Union Trust officer that Loma Linda University had "flipped" our trust and the trusts of 150 other trust holders for no charge. The Columbia Union Trust Services officer answered that the Columbia Union lacked the sophisticated staff and expertise that Loma Linda University had. Fair enough.

But when at the January 21, 2004, meeting in New Jersey, the Union Trust officer chided me for being concerned about the "miserly" $3,667 fee charged us, I suggested that if he asked, perhaps Loma Linda University would make its expertise available to the Columbia Union to flip trusts. He immediately dismissed the suggestion.

Yet, after the sale of our 40-acre property, I learned from a Loma Linda University Trust department attorney that he had spent time advising the individual from the Columbia Union responsible for investing our funds. What does this tell me? Clearly, the Columbia Union was willing to ask for inter-entity cooperation when the Church itself stood to benefit—but not for the benefit of its donors.

The Union Conference's Trust officer's reference to

the "miserly $3,667 fee" charged by their outside attorney troubled me. It reminded me of an observation made by a college classmate who had served as a General Conference auditor. He said, "I have noticed that trustors are more careful in expending trust funds than are trustees."

I was also reminded of a *Business Week* article (December 2003) about "The Top Givers" in the United States. It said these top givers were asking for

1. Measurable results,
2. Efficiency,
3. Transparency, and
4. A business-like rigor in handling their contributions.

But most of all I was reminded of my father's scrupulous handling of the Lord's funds which he was managing.

Before we funded the Columbia Union's Unitrust, I asked the Union Conference if it had qualified people to handle any special technical challenges that we would encounter. I was assured they did, and I took them at their word. What I have just recounted shows that they do not have this expertise.

But when the Columbia Union hired an outside attorney to flip its 16 trusts, the attorney not only charged a hefty fee, he overlooked the fact that our trust was the only one of the 16 funded by real estate, not cash. So, by IRS rules, the Columbia Union was mandated to pay out interest every quarter, starting January 1, 2001—something they did not do.

Both the outside attorney and the Union Conference Trust officer failed to catch the error—undoubtedly because the Union officer is saddled with at least six areas of responsibility. He's admitted as much to me. Why the Columbia Union Conference has not filed a malpractice insurance claim to recoup its losses on this count I will probably never know.

While trying to get answers and extricate myself from this whole comedy of errors, I yearned to be allowed to lay the whole situation before a disinterested group.

I knew about Seventh-day Adventist mediation service, but could never find the information I needed to mobilize it. For several years—ever since the New Jersey Conference turned over management of our apartment house to HOWCO Management Company—I had tried to activate the Dispute Resolution Process on my behalf, only to find that it cannot be used to resolve issues involving trusts.

A senior Church official has suggested that we put all these concerns behind us and simply move forward, and I agree we must move in that direction. But, before moving forward, we need to see corrections, not cover-ups.

Christianity Today, *Adventist Review*, and *Ministry* all stress the need for accountability, candor, openness, honesty, integrity, freedom of information, and transparency. Each of these journals also decries secrecy, conflicts of interest, inappropriate business associations, and misuse of office. How wonderful it sounds! But I simply don't see the practice matching the preaching.

Larry Downing, senior pastor of the White Memorial Church in Los Angeles, teaches ethics in the La Sierra University School of Business and Management. In a recent *Adventist Today* article he told the story of the Glendale Adventist Medical Center respiratory therapist who murdered an unknown number of patients. Downing applauded hospital administrators for their policy of transparency and truthfulness. Other organizations should hear and heed, Downing concludes, including *the Church that shares the name with Glendale Adventist Medical Center.*

An article in the NAD edition of the December 2003 *Adventist Review* informs us that an educational consulting firm hired by Atlantic Union College had advised the then-troubled college that "transparency is just good policy."

It boggles my mind why a Church organization (which teaches the virtues of transparency) should find it necessary to spend money to review the obvious.

If my voice and pen were the only ones calling out

for greater integrity and transparency, I'd suspect the problem was mine, not the Church's. But other dedicated denominational pastors and executives are speaking out just as forcefully.

A West Coast Seventh-day Adventist pastor recently urged me to read the award-winning book *Papal Sin*, authored by committed Catholic historian Gary Wills. Of the protectionism practiced by the Catholic hierarchy, Wills writes:

"These [unethical, secretive] maneuvers are justified by those who think they must shoulder, all alone, the Spirit's role of protecting the Church as necessary measures to protect the mission of Christ. One of the most common objections . . . was the "everybody does it" argument—that is, leaders of every kind have to protect their organizations by stretching or evading or denying the exact truth about it. Those making this defense are the ones . . . in the Church who think it can survive only by acting like any other political body. Admittedly, the rationale for such protective attitudes is different with Church rulers—but only in the sense that they are protecting something more important than any mere earthly authority. This makes playing fast and loose with the truth more, rather than less, justifiable in their eyes . . . covering it up is a crime added to a crime."

After reading the book, I told the Adventist pastor who'd recommended it that Will's condemnation of the Vatican's methods could just as well apply to the Seventh-day Adventist Church.

"Why did you think I asked you to read it?" he chided.

After reading the story of my father's experience with the Church, another denominational employee, an ordained minister with 20 years of service in mission and departmental work, wrote me: "The account of your father's frugal life and extraordinary commitment to his Church is truly inspiring. That his faithfulness was not matched by the stewardship of 'the brethren' in whom he trusted is truly sad. I would like to believe that yours is just an isolated case. But unfortunately my own experience with 'the brethren' and their system leads me to suspect that it is not.

"I agree wholeheartedly with your five reasons for giving. I believe strongly in the concept of 'the priesthood of the believer,' in the principle of stewardship, and in the idea of individual responsibility. After serving my Church for almost two decades as an ordained minister, conference departmental director, and overseas missionary, I have reluctantly concluded that the organization started by the pioneers in the 19th century would astound them today.

"I believe that Christ's parable of the 'Talents' illustrates that the role of a steward involves individual initiative, individual industry, and individual responsibility. And if I am to be a faithful steward, I don't see how I can delegate my responsibility to anyone, even though it might be a relief to do so."

A senior General Conference officer recently wrote me: "I was not surprised, not in the least [by the account of your family's experience with the Church.] Sadly, I could add to it.

"I don't know if I ever told you that I was working on a manuscript dealing with Judas' 30 pieces of silver, postulating that the Church is full of that kind of money, because of faulty morals. Basically, the reason is, I think, because we are increasingly coming to view organization as the Church, i.e. the spiritual body of Christ. We work for the organization before we work for God. It is becoming secular with religious words and phrases. It is a harsh statement, but those rascals (no I don't apologize for the word) you have been dealing with I am sure believe they are doing the organization a great favor.

"They are thinking of the balance sheet and financial report that will prove them efficient stewards. They don't give a thought to God looking and hearing. I could tell you about personal experiences with high-ups I have had to take to task on matters of money . . . I think they truly believe that any amount they can acquire for 'the cause,' almost regardless of how, is in God's own interest, because it is in their interest [and in the] machinery's, called the Church, with the trappings of message. That is the kindest explanation I can give, based on my experience. That means, of course that they do not necessarily see any wrong in it. They are honest crooks."

Recommendations

Instead of ending with a lengthy list of grievances, it seems altogether fitting to offer the following recommendations to help the Church resolve these concerns:

1. Only trained, qualified, and experienced Trust people should handle specialty problems. Too many Trust officers attempt to handle matters that exceed their competency, without adequate understanding of the nuances—personal and technical—of the issues at hand.
2. Detailed, written records should be made of verbal promises. Transcripts of these records should be placed in files, available to succeeding Trust officials. Verbal promises must be written down and preserved inviolate.
3. Manipulation of feeble-minded trustors must forever cease. If "the primary goal of Trust Services representatives it to determine *what the person wants to do*," officers and administrators prone to manipulation of the elderly should be barred from all official interaction with trustors.
4. Showing appreciation is common courtesy. When Trust officers make little or no acknowledgement of gifts, donors assume their gifts are not needed and may turn to causes where the gifts seem better appreciated.
5. Written and verbal inquiries should be acknowledged promptly. A policy of "Freedom of Information"

should be initiated. In a Church projected soon to reach 20 million members, how sad that such acknowledgement can take (in my case) more than three years! A policy of openness and freedom of information would allow a knowledgeable office secretary to handle much of this work.

6. Transparency is the best policy. Conferences should be transparently open and free in sharing information to which members are entitled. Likewise, they should guard the confidentiality of private matters. Too often, in my experience, the opposite is true: for purposes of manipulation, conference leaders withhold that which should be public and publicize that which should be private.

7. Agreements should be kept. Established trust provisions are binding contracts and should be treated accordingly.

8. The Church should spell out the privileges and benefits of membership. The Church apparently has no list of such provisions, though Ellen G. White specifically refers to "privileges and benefits" of membership. These should be listed in the *Church Manual* and taught by evangelists and pastors to prospective new members.

9. Dispute resolution on Church-related financial matters should be available to all Adventists. When Adventists find themselves unable to resolve serious financial disagreements with an entity of the Church, qualified, disinterested mediation should be made available.

10. All levels of the Church, from the local church to the General Conference Committee, would be benefited by instituting secret ballot voting. This will enable laity and ministers to register their opinions on important matters without fearing retribution.

11. A 201-type File similar to that used in the armed services should be devised to track the professional

career of every pastor and administrator and should
be made available to every member at elections.
12. Study the advisability of appointing an "Integrity
Officer" for the Church to help anticipate and resolve
questions of ethics and fairness between members
and the Church, including financial matters.

In Conclusion

Unfortunately, most of the constituency of the Columbia
Union Conference will never learn that they were deprived
of the benefits of as much as $2 million in the matter of my
parents' contributions. Nor will they know of the loss of
$168,000 from Betty's and my contribution.

Our Church should learn to operate with far greater
openness and candor. As matters stand today, when
Church auditors, whose salaries we members pay,
discover irregularities, we (the members of the Church)
are not informed. Rather, the auditors report back to
administrators, probably even to the very administrators
being investigated.

And from my personal experience, it appears that Church
administrators still place little value on the competence of
even the most informed lay participants in denominational
decision-making. I concur completely with the sentiments
of the following letter, published in the November 18,
2003, issue of *Spectrum*: "As we look at our society today,
I would suggest that one of the things that matters most is
the religious voice of the laity. Whatever the tradition—be it
Catholic, Episcopalian, or Adventist—the voice of the laity
is greatly needed. Whatever the votes, actions, or statements
of the organizational Church, it is within the congregations
that policy lives or dies. *The Church is The People.*"

I am further convinced that the Seventh-day Adventist
Church is not "user friendly." My exposure to the gross
inconsistencies between what is preached and what is
practiced causes the deep respect for Church leaders that
had been ingrained in me since childhood, to waver.

Ellen White clearly sums it up, when she writes that if we were more charitable, loving, and kind to one another, there would be 100 in our churches where there is only one today.

I realize that "where your treasure is" there will our hearts be also. And it's in the areas of Christian education and Trust Services—where large amounts of money are at stake—that we see great evidence of cover-ups and defensiveness. Somehow, it's easy to stand tall in the pulpit and cry out for integrity and transparency, until it appears that doing so could hit us, or the Church, in the pocketbook.

If our Church is to be transformed into the kind of organization that will draw new converts by droves and magnetically attract donors to its causes, we must change the way we manage our fund-intensive ministries.

If we can accept the Savior at His word and learn to simply tell the truth—yea, yea, and nay, nav·—regardless of the immediate financial consequences, I believe the Church would be transformed from within.

I won't be around much longer—even if I live to be 105, like Pop. But I'm jealous for my Church and its future! I want to see it empowered, filled with resources, and strong in its mission to the world.

I've shared my story, directly and openly. I've made mistakes in my life—we all have. And it's hard to admit we're not perfect.

But if we can only covenant together to do all in our power to follow the Golden Rule and treat one another as we would treat Jesus Himself, we need never again repeat the kinds of experiences I've shared in these pages.

There is a better way. And by God's grace, we can shoulder the responsibility and master it in our time.

My documented experiences, perhaps, can help move the Church toward that ideal. Tom Mostert, Jr., president of the Pacific Union Conference, writes in the May 2004 North American Division issue of the *Adventist Review*:

"Successful business constantly listens to their customers. They listen for the positive and the negative. Then they do something about the weak areas. The Church must do the same. We need to communicate with each other regularly. Otherwise, frustrations develop and along the way members leave, leaders give up and our mission is neglected. Leaders especially need to hear from those they lead."

Mine and Pop's life experiences encompass most of the past century in Adventism and present a microcosm of where we have come from and where we seem to heading. I was one of the approximately 100 Seventh-day Adventist dentists who graduated from Atlanta-Southern Dental College, under a cooperative agreement between that school and the General Conference.

That group of approximately 100 dentists was largely responsible for initiating interest in establishing the Loma Linda University School of Dentistry. And as I became disillusioned by the lack of forthrightness, freedom of information, secrecy, lack of transparency, and laxness of business rigor in the local and union conferences, my natural philanthropic interests turned toward the Loma Linda University School of Dentistry and the profession I loved.

Since Loma Linda University's (LLU's) Trust Foundation is part of the Adventist Church's Trust Services, where news travels quickly, LLU was no doubt aware of dissatisfaction we had experienced elsewhere in the system.

But I'm pleased to say that our experience donating funds to LLU has been a much more positive experience.

1. First we were assigned our own personal Trust officer, who although responsible to a watchdog committee, is readily available to answer my questions via FAX, email, snail mail, phone, and voicemail.
2. When our Trust officer is unavailable, his personal assistant always returns our calls promptly.
3. Our input has been welcomed and taken seriously.

4. In marked contrast to our past experience, Loma Linda University has never asked us to foot the bill for its legal expenses related to our giving;
5. Our investments have been handled wisely, and both we and the University are benefiting from this careful stewardship;
6. We have been told that soon we will be able to log onto our LLU Trust Foundation stock portfolio via the Internet and track our trust investments on line, just as we do now with our personal Merrill Lynch account.

Has LLU Trust Foundation reached perfection? Not quite. As a boy of 12, I remember hearing a famous missionary tell the story of how she had received large contributions from bandits in China. Why would Jesus (who could extract money from the mouth of a fish) need money unlawfully taken by bandits from needy people? I wondered.

Loma Linda University Trust Foundation has a policy not to accept funds from gambling operations. However, I'm reliably informed that LLU recently found a way to work around that policy and accept a donation from such sources. I wish we could all learn that God really doesn't need our money—the real blessing comes to us, the givers.

A Loma Linda University Trust Services officer recently told me that Trust officers in the past routinely refused phone calls from contributors who wished to share suggestions on how best to market the assets they had contributed.

His first-hand testimony confirms my experience. This calculated non-cooperation between Trust officers and donors works to the disadvantage of both.

On another occasion, while I was visiting the offices of the Loma Linda University Trust Services, my guide showed me a room with about 10 computers where several General Conference auditors were reviewing Trust records. I asked one of the auditors if I, the holder of several trusts with the university, was entitled to receive a copy of the particulars of what the auditors discovered. He assured me that such information was not available to me, but the results would be shared only with the boards of those being audited.

"What a lack of transparency!" I thought. "Their reports are of vital interest to me and my financial contributions help pay their salaries, yet I am not entitled to review their specific findings."

As of this writing, it has now been 15 months since we finalized our last $1.25 million Unitrust with Loma Linda University. We spent considerable time acquainting the first Trust officer assigned to us with the management, marketing, and sale factors related to the Unitrust's assets. But then the Trust officer assigned to us moved to another denominational entity.

A second Trust officer took over and quite recently spent a profitable day on the East Coast with us, studying through the various business ramifications of the Trust's real assets. But then, a couple of weeks later, we received a letter advising us that yet another Trust officer had been assigned to us!

Fortunately, these transitioning officers have communicated well. But past experience has taught us that with the changing of the guard can come loss of significant sums of money. We're uneasy with such rapid changes, and we feel that true professionalism calls for greater stability in the Trust Services workforce. ■

Map of Developed Land

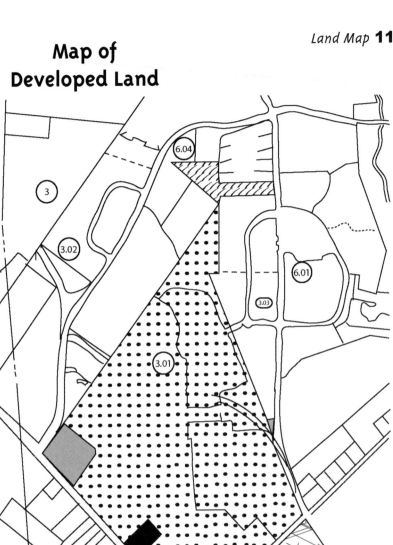

Legend

Five Acres Given to Son (A.C. Koppel) A.C.K. contributed to N.J. Conf. of SDA; Proceeds to go to tithe	*Two Acres* with Residence & Factory. Inherited by A.C.K. at $270,000. Appraised 2004 at $1,240,000	*Ten Acres* C. Koppel gave to Trenton Church. Church sold 3 acres. 7 acres + Church recently appraised at $6,500,000	*Forty Acres* Inherited by A.C.K.; donated to Columbia Union and Loma Linda University	*165 Acres* C. Koppel contributed to N.J. Conf.; sold for $8,250,000

Photos of Developed Land

Karl Koppel constructed this building at a cost of less than $10,000 during the Great Depression as a home for his Universal Knitting Mill.

A large bank and office building now stand on three acres of former Koppel land, for which $500,000 an acre was paid — 10 times more than the Conference had sold them for just a few years before.

These fine homes on former Koppel land are now selling for between $450,000 and $500,000 each.

The new Robbinsville Adventist Church lies on land donated by Karl Koppel. The structure is valued at $6.5 million.

This ornate Washington Town Center office building now stands prominently among other buildings on the 200 acres Karl Koppel once owned.

Robbinsville Adventist Church members received but a fraction of what many had expected to receive from Karl Koppel's final gift. To make up part of the deficit, they sold some of their church property, where this building now stands.

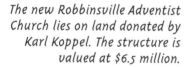

Epilogue . . .

A pre-publication manuscript and an accompanying letter were sent certified mail, return receipt requested, to eight individuals who figure prominently in this book. Signatures of confirmation were received for each of the eight manuscripts sent—in other words, each person to whom it was sent acknowledged receiving the manuscript.

Of the eight, one provided no response; one had his secretary notify us by phone that he found no problems with the manuscript; three sent short letters of protest but pointed out no specific inaccuracies; and, finally, three provided thoughtful responses that informed us of areas in our early drafts that did not present a completely accurate picture.

We thank those who responded—especially those who offered constructive information. They did exactly what we asked them to do in each cover letter. In turn, I am doing exactly what I promised—I have used all credible criticism they have presented in preparing our final draft of this book.

On the next page is the body text of cover letters sent to each of the eight persons who have interacted prominently with the Koppel family and are mentioned specifically (by position, not name) in this book.

August 25, 2004

Dear _____

Enclosed you will find a complete manuscript that contains first-hand references to things I believe you have said, done, and written during my years of interaction with the New Jersey Conference and Columbia Union Conference. This manuscript is not intended primarily as a commentary on the past. Rather, I hope that, when published and marketed independently this fall, its effect will be to urge our Church to markedly improve its treatment of its devout laymen and accord them the Christian courtesy and professionalism which I have often found lacking in my experience with the Church.

In the final paragraph of this letter, you will find a list of the manuscript pages that allude to or quote directly from discussions and interaction you have had with the Koppel family. I trust you will review these passages for accuracy and mail any comments to me by Sept. 15, 2004, at which time our publishing schedule demands that we begin to finalize the manuscript for publication. I have included with this manuscript a stamped, self-addressed envelope for your convenience. If we have not heard from you by Sept. 20, we will assume you have no reason or desire to comment on the manuscript's content.

Sincerely Yours,
Albert C. Koppel, D.D.S.

Results

Response from Associate Editor, Adventist Review:

A voice mail message from the associate editor's secretary said: "He had no problem with the manuscript."

Response from President of Columbia Union Conference:

No answer, either by phone, email, or in writing. Therefore no inaccuracies were pointed out.

Response of Trust Services officer of the Columbia Union Conference:

An answer was received nine days after the September 20, 2004, deadline. No specific inaccuracies were cited. The following *faxed* letter on Columbia Union Conference stationery was received. We have honored his request to remove his name from the manuscript. Also we have followed the advice of several Church officials by referring to him by office, rather than by name.

Dear Al:

I have reviewed the references about me in your manuscript. There are factual inaccuracies and false negative inferences derived from your comments. I therefore request that you delete any and all comments, criticisms, commentaries, critiques, interpretations, observations, and statements about me and if you refuse to delete my name from your manuscript, I request that you include and add this written protest with your manuscript.

I will be happy to discuss this matter with you at your convenience.

Sincerely,
xxxxxxxxxxxxxxxxxx
Trust Services, Columbia Union Conference

Response of President of the New Jersey Conference:

The following letter on New Jersey Conference stationery was received from the New Jersey Conference President.

Dear Dr. Koppel,

I have reviewed the references about me and I dispute the accuracy and the negative inferences derived from your comments. I, therefore, request that you delete any and all comments, criticisms, commentaries, critiques, interpretations, observations, and statements about me, and if you refuse to delete my name from your manuscript, I request that you include and add this written protest to your manuscript.

Sincerely,

xxxxxxxxxxxxxxxxxxx

President, New Jersey Conference

I would have appreciated his listing the factual inaccuracies and false negative inferences as we had requested. None were cited.

No specific inaccuracies were cited. We have, as he

requested, deleted his name from the manuscript. We have included his written protest to the manuscript.

Response of Trust Services officer—New Jersey Conference:

The following letter, written on New Jersey Conference stationery, was received from the New Jersey Conference Trust Services officer. No inaccuracies were cited. We have, as requested, deleted his name from the manuscript. We have added his written (above) protest to the manuscript.

Dear Dr. Koppel,

I have reviewed the references about me and I dispute the accuracy and the negative inferences derived from your comments. I, therefore, request that you delete any and all comments, criticisms, commentaries, critiques, interpretations, observations, and statements about me, and if you refuse to delete my name from your manuscript, I request that you include and add this written protest to your manuscript.

Sincerely,
XXXXXXXXXXXXXXX
Director of Trust Services, New Jersey Conference

Almost a month after our deadline for the return of the manuscript we received from the New Jersey Conference Trust officer a one-sentence letter, along with four pages of documents without accompanying instructions or comments. We are therefore uncertain what specific points this Trust officer intended to make through his response.

Since The New Jersey Conference Trust officer had previously told us that he followed the dictates of his president, we can only surmise that this material was sent at the president's direction. The lots 17 and 23 referred to in his letter constituted the five acres that my wife and I contributed, the proceeds of which we had designated to be applied as tithe.

The enclosed deed for these two lots numbered Lot 17 & 23 has a notation as follows,

"SEE ATTACHED SCHEDULE A"

We found nothing that was labeled SCHEDULE A.

These four pages include a page that is an agreement made and signed by my parents on August 5, 1958, and the then-New Jersey Conference President and Secretary-Treasurer showing that,

1. My parents had deeded 90 acres to the New Jersey Conference,
2. That my parents reserved a "life estate" to the property.,
3. One third of the property was to be allocated to the Trenton Seventh-day Adventist Church,
4. Two thirds of the property was to be allocated to the New Jersey Conference of Seventh-day Adventists.

I do not remember ever having seen this agreement that my parents made with the New Jersey Conference in 1958.

However, the information that directs one third of these assets to the Trenton Church conforms to what I had heard in discussions in our home.

What concerns me is something I have previously

mentioned and bears repeating here. During a visit to my parents' home, a youthful New Jersey Conference Trust Services officer appeared at their home. Before his visit with them, he sat in the car with me and showed me three letters prepared by the then-president of the New Jersey Conference. One letter draft (prepared by the Conference for Pop to sign) authorized a reduction in Pop's gift to the Trenton Church from 33.3 percent to 20 percent; the second letter draft reduced the contribution to the Trenton Church to 15 percent; and the third letter reduced it to 10 percent.

This young Trust officer expressed concern about the propriety of what he had been asked to do. But he pressed forward and visited with my parents that day, presenting the three letters as options for their signatures. I do not know whether my parents signed any of those letters.

But I often wonder: Did the membership of the Trenton Church ever learn about this apparent attempt by their Conference leaders to reduce the benefits Pop had intended for them?

1. Did the Trenton Church get its one-third share?
2. Did my parents sign one of those three letters?
3. Was the share for the Trenton Church reduced to 20%, or 15% or 10%?
4. Why did the former N. J. Conference President attempt to reduce the percentage? These letters were prepared almost 30 years after the agreement was signed that allotted one-third of the proceeds of the land sale to the Trenton Church, and now that Pop was about 100 years old and in failing mental health, it's clear the Conference was urging him to alter those provisions.

In the main text, I have told how Conference officials argued strongly against my request that the proceeds of five acres I donated to the Conference be used to help the Burlington, New Jersey, Church. Did they present the same arguments to Pop, in his advanced age, to try to get him to give less to his home church? I believe they did.

Yet, during this same period of time, the then-General Conference Trust Services director was telling pastors, in print, "Perhaps you have thought of Trust Services as working to direct your members' monies to the conference rather than to your church. You may even have heard of Trust Services representative urging an individual not to leave anything to the local church . . . . " The author then went on to deny that such things were happening any longer in the Church.

Yes, Pop most certainly signed an agreement in 1958 that bequeathed the Trenton Church one third of the value of the property that would be sold at his death.

But a careful reading shows that the drafters of the agreement effectively placed a choke hold on the Trenton Church's use of the funds. For it states, in typical Conference legalese, that the money was to be "used preferably for development of educational facilities, but may be used for other purposes *as the church board, in counsel with the conference administration, sees fit*" (italics mine).

I very much doubt that this is Pop's wording. It appears that because of his total confidence in the brethren, he allowed them to place these constraints on his intended gift to his local congregation.

Response of Former President of New Jersey Conference:

In his written communication, the former president of the New Jersey Conference writes that he at no time dealt with the sale of the property. Betty and I thank him for this now-corroborated information (see below in this Epilogue.) We had been trying to discover who actually had handled that sale.

He further writes, "Contrary to what you have alleged in your composition, in all my dealings with Mr. [Karl]Koppel, I was always very careful not to suggest changes to any of his provisions, but rather to support his wishes and decisions."

This I have trouble accepting, based on what my mother reported to me just hours after this former New

Jersey Conference president visited them and urged Pop to contribute 40 acres which were still titled in hers and Pop's names. I simply cannot see how such behavior concurs with this man's claim that he was "always very careful not to suggest changes to any of his provisions, but rather to support his wishes."

During that same visit, my mother told me, this same man suggested that if my parents wished to leave a portion of the proceeds of those 40 acres to me as an inheritance, the Conference would be glad to direct that to me. This clearly shows that he was indeed leading the conversation, attempting to influence Pop in his old age to do something he had long before decided not to do.

His behavior clearly is at odds with the sentiments of the General Conference Trust Services officer who writes in *Ministry* (February 1, 1991), "The primary goal of the Trust Services representative is to determine what the person wants to do."

But back to the response I received from the former New Jersey Conference president. He writes, "I have always dealt honestly and fairly with you, seeking only to facilitate your wishes and help you to achieve your aims."

This is indeed true—he certainly did assist me, particularly when in his dotage Pop made things difficult when he accused me of stealing his money. Because of Pop's confidence in this former Conference president, this president was able to help persuade Pop, for his own good, to agree to the live with us in our home.

On the other hand, it was this former president who argued strongly to dissuade Betty and me from giving income from the sale of five acres for Burlington Church expense—money we eventually designated as tithe.

This president was there. And I'm positive that he and others present that day in the Conference board room remember that we designated that the funds be used for tithe. Was a written record made of our stipulation? Was the record later lost? What really happened?

The present New Jersey Conference Trust Services officer told me about a year ago that the Conference committee had not yet decided what to do with the proceeds of the sale. Yet, in my view, this is not their decision to make. Betty and I made that decision back in 1986. Did this former Conference president truly do everything he could to help Betty and me achieve our aims? I leave it to the reader to decide.

Response of General Conference Treasurer:

I thank the General Conference treasurer for his lengthy commentary on the first draft of this book. His is by far the most extensive and helpful response. I appreciate his taking my concerns seriously, as evidenced by his having read through the manuscript twice. Betty and I also appreciate his helpful seven-page typewritten response.

The treasurer points out my error in quoting him as saying that the General Conference has no authority over local conferences. What he did say was that the General Conference does not "make" the conferences do things, in a dictatorial way. We took this correction to heart and incorporated it into the current text.

The treasurer also points out that in an early draft, we had assumed the procedures for salary audits were the same as for general audits. The protocols are indeed different. We've clarified this in the current draft.

We have also accepted his suggestion that references to individuals in this book be made only by position—not by name. At first, Betty and I resisted this suggestion—primarily because we feel that by not mentioning names, others holding similar positions in denominational employment may be accused of the unprofessional behaviors we document here—when, in fact they are entirely innocent of such behavior.

During my 40 years of practice, I had to maintain my professional reputation under my own name. I was not generally referred to as "that dentist on Cedar Street." If Church officers may not be named, how can "we" hope to cultivate an informed constituency, capable of making intelligent decisions when we elect officers and other Conference personnel?

The treasurer told me that conference officers are responsible to their executive committees and constituents. Again, if constituents are not privy to the particulars of audits (which I believe is the case) and incidents are not connected with names, how can constituents be expected to provide informed oversight of Conference decisions?

Despite these concerns, however, Betty and I have accepted the treasurer's advice, recognizing that this book is not directed against individuals, but against a system congenitally disposed to secrecy and, yes, deceit. Indeed, our goal may be better served by avoiding focus on individuals and casting them, instead, as the role-players they truly are.

The treasurer also points out that in at least one instance, we seemed to have overstepped factual bounds in interpreting the intent of an individual's words and actions. In our final draft, I have worked especially hard to avoid any improper editorializing in this text.

We understand the treasurer's concerns that the designation of the various parcels of land and their quoted values are, at times, difficult to follow in this book. So, in our final draft, we have worked very hard to make these numbers meaningful, including a map of the properties to help readers visualize the lay of the land.

We also thank the treasurer for correcting our assumption that Trust Services and Education administer the most funds of any two departments in the Church system. The treasurer points out in his letter that the medical work and health food manufacturing actually hold this distinction.

We also appreciate the minor editorial corrections he included in his response. His careful, studied attention to the early drafts has added considerable value to this manuscript.

The treasurer also points out that in our first draft, I often did not include names of persons who seemed critical of some aspect of the Church. My reason for doing so was (and is) to spare these individuals possible vindictive treatment. I distinctly recall, for example, how theologian M.L. Andreassen in the 1950s was stripped of his retirement benefits because some of his views differed from those of some leading brethren.

While I realize that this type of retribution is no longer practiced, I do believe that dissidents are still persecuted in significant, though perhaps more subtle, ways.

The treasurer also counseled us that some of the concerns mentioned in this book could be resolved with "a few minutes of two-way conversation." I couldn't agree more! In I Corinthians 6:5 we read, "Is it so, that there is not a wise man among you? no, not one that shall be able to judge between his brethren?"

For at least 10 years before beginning to write this book, I worked hard to try to work through my concerns with the Church. I wrote letters, I phoned, I traveled long and far, I asked for mediation—to no avail. If leaders are not willing to follow the very biblical advice they dispense to their constituents, it's no wonder we have problems.

I wish to assure the treasurer that it is indeed all right with me if he phones me after Annual Council (October 2004 and still waiting).

In his Sept. 15, 2004 letter, the General Conference treasurer says, "I have not been sure how to best find a positive resolution to this matter."

His answer baffles me! The question is so simple: "What do the records of the New Jersey Conference show regarding what the proceeds of the sale of the five acres we contributed would benefit?"

It's been five years since I first asked this question—and I've asked it of every level of Church structure. I do have one letter from the New Jersey Conference Trust Services officer, most likely written at the direction of his conference president, telling me that the conference has not yet decided how to use the proceeds.

The General Conference treasurer has written me a letter in which he states, "There are occasions when the officers of the organization directly involved *feel* they have responded adequately." That may well be. But it conveys the destructive message to constituents, "We, the officers—not you!—will decide whether or not your donation will be used as tithe!"

I have yet to hear a practicing Seventh-day Adventist object to the biblical *principle* of tithe paying. On the other hand, I have heard many, many complaints about how the Church *uses* tithe funds. From experience I am compelled to conclude that those complaints have merit!

Response from the former New Jersey Conference Trust Services director:

We thank the former New Jersey Conference Trust Services director for his detailed, nuanced critique of the manuscript. We especially appreciate his clear statement that it was he who chaired the committee that administered the sale of Pop's 165 acres. We had been trying for some time to pinpoint who actually directed that sale. Others had reported that it was the Columbia Union Trust Services officer. It seemed impossible to get a clear answer. Now we know.

We also thank this former New Jersey Trust officer for his sentiments that I should spare myself the "embarrassment of publishing an inaccurate portrayal" of events surrounding the donation of the various properties. To the extent that he has provided accurate information that has helped us prepare a more credible book, we thank him.

I personally regret that he included in his critique the

following statement: "I am truly hurt by your judgment about my motives in serving you." The incident referenced does not appear in the finalized draft of the book. In all areas where I have appeared to write critically of some individuals and their motives, I honestly have bent every effort to give them every benefit of the doubt.

In his critique, he also points out that the Trust Services of the Adventist Church has contracted with the US Trust Company to manage trust agreements. This is good news! However, I have not yet been advised that our own trust agreement is being managed by this impressive firm. I hope it is!

He also tells us that the Columbia Union Conference had qualified staff to handle larger donations— an assertion we continue to contest. In this book, we confine our criticism to the marketing techniques employed by the Church, not the handling of legal matters of the sale (which with one exception were handled in an orderly fashion.) We continue to defend the view that faulty and less than savvy marketing procedures led to the loss of at least $2 million to the Church in the sale of the five and 165 acres. This argument is clearly articulated on pages 48 - 57.

He is correct in stating that a Realtor who eventually received $400,000 from the sale of 165 donated acres did not represent himself as Pop's agent of record, and we apologize for so stating in an earlier draft. However, we still stand by our position that the payment of the $400,000 Realtor's fee was a mistake. (For a full explanation, please see pages 52 - 54.

This former New Jersey Conference Trust officer also indicates that in final stages of the sale of the 165 acres, the Conference became concerned with the complexity of the offers being presented, including the detailed contractual language. I can understand these concerns, as we went through the same experience in the later sale of 40 adjacent acres. The agreement of sale for the 40 acres required nearly 20 corrections and revisions before we finalized the deal.

I appreciate this Trust officer's concern that I not be embarrassed by making unsustainable assertions in this book. Following his counsel, I have redoubled my efforts to document every fact I present.

Yet, we have been hampered at times in this quest by lack of freedom of information in the Church, lack of transparency, secrecy, unanswered letters, and stonewalling.

Several factual errors noted by this former Trust officer in an earlier draft were the result of our inability to obtain this information, because of the chilling climate of defensiveness we found among Church leaders.

Again, we have spared no effort to carefully and accurately present my concerns in this book. We shared our first draft with each and every living player in this real-life drama, and several of them showed the grace to offer helpful advice and provide factual information.

We have worked exceedingly hard, and at considerable financial expense, to ensure the accuracy and balance of what is written in this book. Once again, we thank all who have helped—especially our critics—in its preparation. It hasn't been easy for any of us. ∎